This book is published to accompany the television series entitled
Strictly Come Dancing, first broadcast on BBC1 in 2012.

Executive Producers – Glenn Coomber and Andrea Hamilton
Series Producer – Leanne Witcoop

10 9 8 7 6 5 4 3 2 1

Published in 2012 by BBC Books, an imprint of Ebury Publishing.
A Random House Group Company

BBC Books would like to thank Glenn Coomber, Andrea Hamilton, Leanne
Witcoop, Jane Atkinson , Claire Bridgland, Kim Winston, Richard Curwen,
Richard Halliwell and the rest of the *Strictly Come Dancing* Production team.

Strictly Come Dancing logo ™ & © BBC 2012. BBC logo ™ & © BBC 1996.
Devised by the BBC and Licensed by BBC Worldwide Limited.
Text by Alison Maloney
Introductions by Sir Bruce Forsyth and Tess Daly
Copyright © Woodlands Books Ltd 2012

The Random House Group Limited Reg. No. 954009

Addresses for companies within the Random House Group can be found at
www.randomhouse.co.uk

A CIP catalogue record for this book is available from the British Library.

ISBN 978 1 84990583 1

The Random House Group Limited supports The Forest Stewardship Council
(FSC®), the leading international forest certification organisation. Our
books carrying the FSC label are printed on FSC® certified paper. FSC is the
only forest certification scheme endorsed by the leading environmental
organisations, including Greenpeace. Our paper procurement policy can
be found at www.randomhouse.co.uk/environment

Commissioning editor: Lorna Russell
Project editor: Sarah Watling
Design: Karin Fremer
Production: Antony Heller

Series 9 photography by Guy Levy © BBC 2011; Series 10 photography
by Guy Levy © BBC 2012; Rehearsal photography by Guy Levy © Woodlands
Books Ltd; Live Tour photography © Alfie Hitchcock, courtesy of Strictly Come
Dancing Live Tour; all other photography © Getty images and Corbis.

Colour origination by: Altaimage, London
Printed and bound in Germany by Mohn Media GmbH

To buy books by your favourite authors and register for offers,
visit www.randomhouse.co.uk

The Official 2013 Annual

Alison Maloney

BBC BOOKS

CONTENTS

An introduction from Bruce and Tess 8

STAGE ENTERTAINMENT AND PHIL McINTYRE ENTERTAINMENT
IN ASSOCIATION WITH BBC WORLDWIDE PRESENT

BBC

Strictly Come Dancing
THE LIVE TOUR

★★★★★

'SUPREMELY ELEGANT, THE AUDIENCE ADORED EVERY SECOND'

MAIL ON SUNDAY

★★★★★

'THE ULTIMATE FEEL GOOD SHOW'

DAILY TELEGRAPH

TICKETS ON SALE NOW!

Date	Venue	Phone
18 - 20 January	**BIRMINGHAM** NIA	0844 338 8000
22 - 24 January	**NEWCASTLE** Metro Radio Arena	0844 493 6666
25 - 27 January	**GLASGOW** SECC	0844 395 4000
29 - 30 January	**LIVERPOOL** Echo Arena	0844 8000 400
31 January - 1 February	**MANCHESTER** Evening News Arena	0844 847 8000
2 - 3 February	**LONDON** O2 Arena	0844 856 0202
5 - 6 February	**LONDON** Wembley Arena	0844 815 0815
7 - 8 February	**NOTTINGHAM** Capital FM Arena	0844 412 4624
9 - 10 February	**SHEFFIELD** Motorpoint Arena	0114 256 56 56

strictlycomedancinglive.com ★ facebook.com/strictlylive

A MESSAGE FROM

SIR BRUCE FORSYTH

As we go into our tenth series, I still have wonderful memories of last year's *Strictly Come Dancing*. How could Forsyth foresee that Russell Grant was going to be such a star? It amazed everybody – especially me, and for the first six weeks people were tuning in just to see what he got up to. I'll never forget him being fired out of that canon … I never knew he had such a short fuse.

In the end, Harry was an excellent winner. What I didn't know about Harry until quite a way into the series was that, because he's a drummer, he memorised the routines by translating every step into a drum beat. So to him, it wasn't only dancing, it was a piece of drum music. What a clever idea.

But Harry wasn't the only talented competitor last year. It was incredible how Chelsee gradually blossomed and she was so humble about how good her dancing became. And of course there was Jason, a great performer who kept up a high standard from week one.

Lastly, I have to mention someone who didn't quite make the Final - Nancy Dell'Olio. Who else could step out a coffin the way Nancy did? She was an awful dancer but she didn't know it! She carried it all off in her own way and she loved all the dresses and sparkle. Mind you, I still don't know what Anton really thought!

At the beginning, the contestants don't know whether they can dance or not, but they soon get into it and often surprise themselves. It shows that anyone with a little co-ordination can dance. There are many people walking round the streets who don't realise that they could be good ballroom dancers.

Last year, we went to Wembley for the first time. I have to admit I was very nervous because of the size of the crowd and the place itself. In the end I had nothing to worry about. It was a fantastic experience and gave me the courage to play the Albert Hall in May 2012 doing all the things I love to do as an all round entertainer. It was one of the greatest nights of my life. Here I was, at 84, a variety artist, performing a One Man Show at The Royal Albert Hall! Thankfully, behind me was Dave Arch and a 30-piece orchestra of the finest musicians in the land. I can't wait to go back there. If I thought that was a big audience, a few weeks later I played to 30,000 people at the Hop Farm Festival in Kent, and without Wembley, I never would have done either.

Which brings me to the singers, who are featured in the pages of this book. The singers, like Dave Arch and his orchestra, are amazing. The way they sing live week after week in such a variety of different styles is a joy to listen to and I admire them and all the musicians so very much.

This year, we have a new judge, the lovely Darcey Bussell. What a pleasure to welcome someone so revered in the dancing world to the show. I wish her so much luck.

One final thing. Apparently, quite a few people wrote in last year saying they missed the dance off, so it's back. When push comes to shove …. we're here to please!

Here's to another fantastic series. Enjoy.

OVER TO YOU, TESS

The tenth series has arrived and this year's line-up is shaping up to be the fittest cast – and not just in the looks department. We've got two Olympic athletes, a cricketer and some West End stars, so on paper this looks like the most dynamic line-up ever.

It is a great mixture of personalities, and watching the group dance on the launch show you could already see the potential. Denise and Kimberley were amazing. They both have some West End experience. Denise starred in *Chicago* but it's ten years since she's danced and she's given birth since, so she hasn't had much call for high-kicking recently! Glamour-wise she's says she is going to Essex it up – with false eyelashes, the make-up, the diamante and sequins. I'm not sure if that's a threat or a promise.

Louis Smith is going to take the routines to a whole new level because from the gymnastic side of things, nobody can touch him. Even the pros are standing there with their mouths open! He somersaulted through the air during his very first outing on the dance floor – it was just incredible.

Many contestants find seven hours a day of training overwhelming, but Victoria and Louis come straight from the Olympics so for them it's water off a duck's back. They might struggle with the entertainment side of it, and Louis was terrified before the first dance, but a lot of sports stars do well because they have the stamina and discipline. With these two, even the professionals might struggle to keep up.

Victoria looked stunning in her *Strictly* sequinned two-piece costume. There wasn't much of it but she wore it well and I'm currently obsessed by her washboard abs!

To add to our cast of characters we've got the girlband vs. the boyband, with Girls Aloud and Westlife and we've got Dani Harmer from CBBC. My seven-year-old daughter Phoebe and her friends are really excited about Dani – and let's not forget it's the kids who tell mums and dads what they want to watch on Saturday night. Then we have our supermodel, Jerry Hall – the fashion diva, one eyebrow arched, strutting across the floor like it's a catwalk. She's hilariously witty and she just doesn't give a damn. Jerry isn't used to censoring what she says, so there may be a few apologies on the live show this year. She's also six foot in her stocking feet so in heels she'll be towering over Anton and I've got a feeling she'll be wearing the trousers! The joker has finally found his queen!

I must speak to Zoe Ball and tell her just how much I love her dad. Johnny is adorable. He's our oldest contestant ever, and you wouldn't know it. He's ageless because he's so full of the joys of life and of dancing and he's skipping round like a giddy schoolboy. He's so endearing, you just want to hug him.

This year we have Darcey, our new lady judge. She's an iconic dancer and brings such credibility to the panel. She will be the rose among the thorns, keeping the boys in order. I have pre-warned her they need a lot of discipline, so don't be afraid to show them a firm hand. They expect it and perhaps even welcome it. Especially Bruno – reign him in!

WHAT'S NEW?

Like the dancers on the show, *Strictly Come Dancing* never stands still for long. This year it is in the hands of executive producers Andrea Hamilton and Glenn Coomber, but they promise there will be no huge shocks for the devoted audience.

'I think there is a wonderful familiarity to the show that the audience enjoys,' says Glenn. 'The moment we took the job we accepted that this is not our show, it is the viewers' show. They own it, they know it better than we will ever know it, so we were very conscious of not coming in and making sweeping changes that will make the show unfamiliar.'

Instead, the new team plan to build on the huge success of series nine and tweak, rather than overhaul, the best bits.

'We can see where it works and therefore what to push further, and we know the odd thing that didn't work,' explains Andrea. 'The changes you'll see this time round are a focus back on the training, while in the results show you'll see more Claudia Winkleman backstage. There are always things that can be enhanced, no matter how brilliant.'

The biggest change to the format this year is the return of the dance off, axed in series eight. 'It was missed by the audience,' reveals Andrea. 'It was good

to try a different way and it opened the results show up to some interesting items, like Len's Lens. We're keeping the relaxed feel of the results show but instead of a second pro dance the second bit of dancing you'll see is the dance off.'

Last year, the Grand Final took place in Blackpool's famous Tower Ballroom but for series ten, for the first time in four years, there will be no Blackpool run. 'It's a logistical thing, because it costs a lot of money to get up there,' says Glenn. 'And for us it is quite exciting that we're doing it at Television Centre, because it will be the last live *Strictly* to come from there before the building is closed. There's a bit of nostalgia there and it will be very special.'

Wembley week, in aid of Children in Need, will once again take place in November and the themed nights, including the scarily popular Halloween show, stay in place. The professional line up has only one change, with Karen Hauer replacing Kalya Virshilas, and former ballerina Darcey Bussell has joined the judging panel.

'Our cast of dancers is great and Karen is a brilliant addition to it,' says Glenn. 'Darcey makes up the strongest dance panel we've ever had. Her knowledge is phenomenal. And she'll keep the boys in check.'

'Darcey is incredibly knowledgeable and a really warm and lovely person,' adds Andrea.

Changes this year include: a new dancer, Karen, (right) and a move from Blackpool (opposite page) for the final.

Fans can still look forward to a Halloween-themed show in series ten.

Prima ballerina, Darcey Bussell, joins *Strictly* as the new judge.

INTRODUCING
Darcey

After a stint as guest judge in 2009, Darcey Bussell is back on the judging panel on a more permanent basis. Here is a little background on our dancing diva.

Widely recognised as the most accomplished English ballerina of all time, *Strictly's* new judge Darcey Bussell was a late starter when it came to dance. Although she began Saturday ballet classes at five, she only went because her friends were there and she 'used to hide under the piano'.

She went on to attend the Arts Educational School in the Barbican, where she showed a flair for dance, and then to the Royal Ballet School at White Lodge at 13, two years after most of her classmates.

'It took me a while to get passionate about it,' she admits. 'I went to the ballet school late so I had a lot of catching up to do. I didn't believe I was able to achieve anything. But after a year or so of being at the school, I finally said, "This has to be my life. It's my world now."'

Her first stage appearance, at the age of 11, did little to encourage the dancing bug. 'I was a stork and I had to do a little routine but every time I turned around I would whack somebody with my beak!' she laughs. 'I remember being terrified I was going to hurt somebody.'

After putting in the extra hours in the dance studio, and training through her summer holidays, Darcey was accepted into the Royal Ballet's Upper School at 16. This led to the lead role in *The Prince of the Pagodas* and in 1989, at the age of 20, she became The Royal Ballet's Principal Dancer, the youngest ballerina to be given the honour.

Since then Darcey has become a household name and starred in numerous ballets, as well as dancing at the Queen Mother's 90th Birthday celebrations in 1990. She was awarded an OBE in 2005 and CBE in 2006 and has made many TV appearances, including classic cameos with Dawn French on *French and Saunders* and *The Vicar of Dibley*.

Darcey, who is married to banker Angus Forbes and is mum to Phoebe, 11, and eight-year-old Zoe, retired in 2007 and says her proudest achievement is performing after the birth of her girls.

'I never believed after having my second baby that I would perform for another three years,' she says. 'It was not a conventional life. I took my kids on tour with me when they were young, and that was hard, but it put things in perspective and I was suddenly proud of my job and what I was able to achieve.'

More recently, Darcey came out of retirement to dance at the closing ceremony of the 2012 London Olympics.

'It was such a buzz,' she says. 'Two weeks of athletics created the perfect build-up for the closing ceremony and having the athletes in the arena with us was so exciting. It was their celebration of everything they had achieved in those two weeks, so there was a party feeling. It was one of those days when you think that nothing will ever match this.'

Opposite page: Darcey performing in *The Sleeping Beauty;* **left: Darcey dances with Johnathan Cope in The** *Prince of the Pagodas;* **centre: meeting the Queen in 2002; right: with** *The Vicar of Dibley* **star, Dawn French.**

THE STORY OF SERIES 9

Lady and the Champ

Week one was split into two shows, with no evictions. Holly Valance kicked off the series with a cheeky cha-cha-cha after admitting that being teamed with champ Artem was 'boggling my marbles'. Len told her 'It's not the best first dance I've seen – but it's close.' But Dan Lobb failed to make a good first impression with a 'wooden' waltz and bad boy Robbie Savaged the cha-cha-cha, earning a 2 from Craig.

Russell Comes Out of His Shell

After revealing he hadn't danced for years because he was 'too fat', stargazer Russell Grant emerged as Botticelli's *Venus* for the campest cha-cha-cha ever seen on *Strictly*. 'It's like watching Frankie Howerd do Bananarama,' marvelled Bruno. Singer Lulu was nothing to 'Shout' about after messing up the steps of the same dance in what Craig called a 'Dance Dis-ah-ster.'

First Bout for Judges

The regular rows between Craig and Len took on a violent edge after the acerbic Aussie called Audley's hands 'spatulistic' and awarded him a 2. Len told the beefy boxer, 'do me a favour – as you walk by, punch Craig.' Anita began her dancing day with an L on her back, but made it stand for Lady, as she delivered an elegant waltz and ended the night sharing first place with Holly.

Harry Drums Up Support

In order to get drummer Harry Judd to feel the rhythm of the cha-cha-cha, Aliona handed him his drumsticks to hold during training. 'I do feel more at home with my sticks in my hand,' he admitted. He impressed with a solid 28, although he sparked a row between the judges, with Len calling Craig 'a nasty piece of work' for saying the dance was 'too placed'.

Chelsee Calling

A frustrated Pasha confiscated his partner's phone after complaining, 'Chelsee gets distracted so easily, it's unbelievable.' The high-energy salsa that followed went down a storm with the judges, scoring 29, and Alesha told her it was 'fun, flirty and fearless'. Rory channelled Sean Connery for his 'Shexy Shalsha' but Craig compared him to 'rat on a sticky strip'.

Alex Swings to the Left

The *One Show* host had a shocking time in training, after mean partner James electrocuted her every time she got her left and right mixed up. But she was the one handing out the shocks during her foxtrot – by sitting on the lap of Labour peer John Prescott and planting a smacker on his cheek. Jason's foxtrot proved red hot as he scooped 33 points and the top of the leader board.

Nance in her Pants

Italian temptress Nancy attempted to up her salsa scores by flirting with Len before climbing on the desk and shaking her rear in his face. The saucy judge said, 'the most exciting part was when I took a crafty glance up your dress', and Nancy finished bottom of the table with a combined score of 26. The public saved her and Edwina lost her *Strictly* seat.

Dramatic Licence

Broadway Week brought high drama with Holly getting her heel caught during her smouldering *Chicago* jail tango, while still rattling Len and Bruno's cage; Rory finding his feet with an elegant Top Hat and Tails quickstep and Audley tripping over his size 17 feet. Lulu and Brendan caused a stir with an illegal lift in their *Phantom of the Opera* rumba, with Craig marking them down and rulebook stickler Len, surprisingly, jumping to their defence.

Battle of Two Camps

Self-appointed 'High Priest of Camp' Russell was advised to get more 'masculine' for the foxtrot – by Craig! But Aussie Jason outdid them both by going back to his *Priscilla* days and donning his stage costume of feathers and cat-suit to introduce Kristina to the musical's famous bus before delivering a schizophrenic tango which went, as Bruno put it, from 'strong, powerful, aggressive' to 'camp as Christmas' and scored four 9s.

Dan Lobbed Out

Breakfast presenter Dan and partner Katya attempted an elegant Viennese waltz to Queen's track 'Someone To Love'. Sadly no-one loved the dance and Craig told him, 'you have an awkward nature about you generally.' While Nancy and Anton's tango to Nine number 'Be Italian' scored lowest, with 20, the two couples faced the public vote and *Daybreak's* Dan faced his last *Strictly* sunset.

Jason Meets his Waterloo in Chelsee

Chelsee had a busy week, squeezing rehearsals around filming on *Waterloo Road* in Rochdale and even dancing on set, dressed as a bride. But all the air miles she and Pasha put in paid off with a high-flying airport-themed quickstep. Craig called it 'First Class' and the firecracker knocked Jason off the top spot for the first time and even beat Harry – who got the first ten of the series for his waltz.

Audley's Ballet Bout

After Natalie suggested ballet would help his foxtrot, Audley protested 'I'm a boxer, I don't do ballet.' But a spell at the bar knocked him into shape and he admitted, 'It's made me more graceful.' Even Craig saw the improvement, despite a hiccup when Natalie's dress snapped mid-dance. But the Aussie judge upset James when he called Alex's rumba 'sexless, cold and stiff' and gave her a 4.

Lasting Impression

Craig's criticism of Lulu's samba caused a furious response from Brendan and when James waded in, Len told him to 'Turn up, keep up and shut up!' Rory struggled to get sexy for the cha-cha-cha and told Erin, 'I'm wired wrong. You press the butch button you get camp.' Bruno compared him to a 'cocky rooster strutting around the yard,' but the laughter turned to tears when the disappointed comic was voted off.

Spooky Celebs

There were plenty of tricks and treats on Halloween week as the whole cast appeared as the Addams Family and even got the judges in on the act, clicking their fingers to the theme tune. Lulu's paso doble got off to a flying start as she descended from the rooftops with batwings to the strains of 'Highway to Hell' and Holly's *Black Swan* routine was declared 'magnificent' by Alesha.

Dance Horror

Craig got the fright of his life when Robbie jumped on the desk at the end of his paso, thrusting his hips. 'I could have done without all the lascivious hip thrusts,' he said. 'And particularly the end one in my face!' But there was real horror for Chelsee, who was left in tears when her dress came down during a tango. But Bruno assured her 'This wicked little witch is a wicked little dancer.'

Creatures of the Night

Russell's samba brought out the devil in him, Harry got his fangs out for a tasty tango and Audley met Audrey in the *Little Shop of Horrors*. Jason 'Bewitched' the judges into a score of 37 to top the board and Nancy stole the show by climbing out of a crystal encrusted coffin. Bruno told her, 'you dance like the walking dead' and it was curtains for the Queen of the Night.

Lord of the Ring

Russell brought the Spanish bullring to the dance floor, starting his paso doble on a mechanical steed. 'Demented and fabulous,' said Bruno while Craig simply deadpanned, 'astonishing'. It didn't keep him from the bottom of the leader board but the public loved it and he lived to fight another day. Olé!

Week 6

It's Not Where You Start, It's Where You Finish

Alex and James scored an elegant quickstep which 'packed a punch', according to Craig but it almost ended in disaster when Alex's heel caught in her dress and the final notes saw them fall into a heap onto the floor. Harry got his guns out for the samba, leaving the judges hot under the collar, with Bruno praising his 'pecs appeal' and Anita delivered a sparkling charleston, which Alesha dubbed 'light, cute, fun.'

Craig Takes the Chair

With Len taking a rare week off, Craig was in the head judge hotseat and *Dirty Dancing* star Jennifer Grey stepped in as guest judge. She put Chelsee in a flap after her charleston when she said, 'from one Baby to another – if you keep dancing like that nobody's going to put you in the corner.' Lulu tried to curry favour with a smacker for the new head, but the public gave her the kiss off.

Better the Devil You Know

After falling down to the middle of the table in week 6, with a disappointing 28 for his rumba, Jason received a message from famous ex Kylie Minogue. 'I've been watching you and you still look every bit as good as you did 23 years ago,' she said. 'You're doing fantastically well.' The boost did him good and Jason was back on form with a stunning Viennese waltz and 35 points.

Week 7

Arrrrgh-tem

Having made it through the jive with a serious back injury, Russian stoic Artem was forced to duck the rumba on medical advice. Valiant knight Brendan stepped in to help out and landed Holly an impressive 34 points, with Craig saying, 'I am loving this new partnership.' Robbie also scored with the judges, grabbing his record high with 31 for the American smooth.

Anita Gets Serious

Harry's tango caused a row after Len declared it 'too clinical' and his fellow judges disagreed, with Alesha suggesting he was 'jet-lagged.' With two 10s Harry topped the table and even Craig was one up on Len's mark of 8. Bubbly Anita struggled not to smile during the Argentine tango and, despite her best score, ended up in the bottom two. But it was boxer Audley that was KO'd in the vote.

Wembley Week

The couples were given a pep talk by former England manager Graham Taylor before their big night at Wembley, for Children in Need, and Anita's hubby, Brian May, got the evening off to a right royal start with a Queen medley. The fearsome foursome joined in with a recreation of the famous 'Bohemian Rhapsody' video – and Bruno showed he could do the fandango by dancing on the judges' desk. Scaramouche!

Russell Gets Fired

Alex jumped for joy after Craig told her he was 'seeing some improvement' in her tango. An 'overwhelmed' Jason messed up his otherwise perfect jive and Chelsee topped the table after a spectacular jive. Russell reached for the stars when he was shot out of a cannon and Craig was booed when he commented, 'Dumbo springs to mind!' But the stargazer was given the rocket in the public vote.

Hats Off To Alex

Alex and James changed headgear three times in a spirited charleston but James blew his top hat after Craig called the dance 'mediocre' and the couple scored 29. 'This girl has never danced before,' he fumed. 'She went out and sold it.' Holly was hot to foxtrot with a routine that Bruno called, 'Breathtaking, sexy, hot.' And Chelsee scored 35 for a tango, despite Bruno's telling her, 'I want you to be badder.'

Good Knight Anita

Jason's charleston was declared 'truly fabulous' by Len but Harry trumped it with a dashing quickstep, earning three 10s – then went on to win the swingathon. Robin was out of action with a foot infection and chivalrous Brendan stepped in to partner Anita. The Duchess of Cornwall turned up at rehearsals and told the actress, 'You are a wonderful example to our generation.' But Anita was knocked out after scoring 30 for her cha-cha-cha.

Movie Magic

The quarter finals had a film theme and there was plenty of Hollywood glamour on the dance floor. Bruno said *Pretty Woman* Alex was 'gorgeous' in her American smooth while 'Spanish sorceress' Holly got two 10s for her fiery *Zorro* paso doble. Chelsee wanted to be a screen princess for the jive and went green when it turned out to be *Shrek*'s Fiona. But she got a fairytale ending with a top score of 39.

Savage Cuts

Harry's *Robin Hood* rumba stole the hearts of the judges, with Alesha calling it, 'touching, sensitive, romantic.' Jason performed a 'Singing in the Rain' routine which saw him using an umbrella to lift partner Kristina and had Craig complaining, 'It's getting boring now. Everyone's good!' Robbie was Mr Blond in what Alesha described as 'one cool quickstep.' Jason and Robbie were in the bottom two and the Welsh footie star was sent off.

Week 11

Chelsee Power Show

After an elegant American smooth Chelsee turned passionate for a storming paso doble which knocked the judges' socks off. 'Paso personified,' said Craig. 'Gob-smackingly good.' It was Chelsee's turn to be gobsmacked when she landed the first perfect score of the series. Jason was hot on her tail, though, with four 10s for a steamy Argentine tango that was like a fight to the death and had Alesha jumping out of her seat in excitement.

Alex is Swept Away

Presenter Alex scored 34 for her semi-final waltz as Bruno dubbed her 'the belle of the ball'. She began her salsa dressed as a charwoman in a brown overall wielding a broom and Bruno purred, 'you can come and scrub my floor any time.' A combined score of 65, however, couldn't save her from the public vote and Alex was the first of two celebs to get the brush off.

Not So Jolly Holly

An exhausted Holly was in tears in training as she struggled to learn the two dances but she and Artem gave the charleston a modern twist, starting behind DJ decks and delivered a stunning Argentine tango which scored 36 and had Alesha telling her, 'You really are a contender.' Sadly there were more tears when she was voted out. Harry topped the table, in spite of Jason and Chelsee's perfect scores, and all three went through to live final.

The Grand Final

The live final moved to the Tower Ballroom for the first time and it really made Blackpool rock. Jason revived his *Priscilla* tango as the judges' choice and landed a perfect score. He promised a 'showbiz' showdance and he delivered. 'It was a showbiz extravaganza! A theatrical spectacular!' said Bruno. Another 40 put the showman at the top of the bill but it was curtains in the public vote.

Week 12

Chelsee gets the Blues

The 'pocket rocket' blasted off with a repeat of the *Shrek* jive that won her a score of 39 and followed it with a showdance full of dangerous lifts, which Len called, 'bright and shiny like the Blackpool illuminations.' In the second show she went head to head with Harry with a rumba that Craig dubbed 'absolutely magnificent' and a repeat of the airline quickstep which earned her 39 points.

The Boy with the McFlying Feet

Harry received his first full score for the 'stunning' quickstep and got his guns out, as Aliona ripped his sleeves off, for a Rock 'n'Roll showdance to 'Great Balls of Fire'. An American smooth to 'Can't Help Falling in Love' struck a chord with Alesha and Craig who both declared their love for the dreamy drummer after his stunning Argentine tango. The nation agreed and Harry and Aliona lifted the glitterball as *Strictly* champs.

Wild about
HARRY

There were no McFlys on Harry Judd when it came to bagging the *Strictly* trophy. The dashing drummer certainly found his rhythm by the end of the ninth series, when he beat his retreat with the trophy held high. But there was one person he couldn't convince of his dancing ability – himself.

'The first time I thought I was any good was three months after *Strictly* had finished,' he confesses. 'I decided to watch a few of the dances on the internet, and I thought, 'Aah, you were pretty good.'

'When I was in the show, I was so self-critical. On the first week my friends came and watched me and said I was great so I was really excited, but when I watched it I was genuinely embarrassed because it was so bad.

'I went into training the next day with the determination to do better and then the following week, I thought, "That was pretty poor." I'm obsessive and I'm a perfectionist but those two character traits served me well.'

Being the drummer of pop band McFly, Harry already had rhythm and had won a Children in Need special against Saturdays star Rochelle Wiseman. But his first taste of the *Strictly* experience proved more of a hindrance than a help.

'I enjoyed the Children in Need thing but when I finished it I thought, 'I'm glad that's over. I'm never doing that again.' It was so stressful. When I was asked to do the show I said "No, I'm not going to do it.' But even then I knew, deep down, that I would. I couldn't resist the challenge.'

Despite his own reservations, Harry immediately caught the eye of professional Anton Du Beke, who swapped the glitterball for a crystal ball at the start of the series.

'Anton nicknamed me "champ" before he'd even seen me dance,' laughs Harry. 'He and James were teasing me saying "You'll win, you're the champ," but I was just hating it, thinking, "This is so unfair, I'm going to be awful." It was a bit of banter but it put the pressure on.'

Harry threw himself into intense training with partner Aliona but hard work couldn't calm the first-night nerves.

'I was terrified,' he recalls. 'I was so scared and I don't know quite how I got through it. The feeling of just finishing the dance was just incredible. But the nerves don't get any better, unfortunately. It was nerve-wracking every week.'

Nerves aside the little drummer boy got off to a strong start with a cha-cha-cha that earned him 28 points. His scores climbed into the 30s by week three, but he stayed one step behind Jason Donovan on the leader board until week seven. Then came his breakthrough dance.

'I clicked with the Argentine tango, which I thought really suited me and I felt, 'I could do that', he says. 'It only took us a couple of days to learn it really and that was such a relief because it was quite a stressful week.'

Harry 'clicked' with the Argentine tango which put him top of the leaderboard for the first time.

Craig told the delighted dancer, 'It was filth and I LOVED it' and Bruno was beside himself, declaring, 'It was moodier than a thunderstorm in the pampas. You've never been stronger, you've never been more attractive.' With two tens, he topped the board for the first time.

Two weeks later he was on top again, with a near-perfect quickstep and full points for the swingathon. 'Apart from winning the trophy my favourite moment was winning the swingathon. It came at the end of a very stressful week for Aliona, when we were learning the quickstep, and I wasn't looking forward to it but I really enjoyed it and it turned out as one of my best dances. I didn't think I'd win the swingathon as well so it was great.'

The 26-year-old star does admit to some low moments – and says the party was almost over with the samba. 'There's a lot of hippy stuff and you've got to let go and try and be sexy. I really struggled with that so it took me the longest to learn. My patience was wearing thin, and I kept thinking, "I've got to do this in front of millions of people, and I literally can't do it." It wasn't until the Friday before the show that I got it so Saturday was really touch and go.'

He pulled through and kept up the standard to the final. Eyeing up the competition Harry found it was anybody's game.

Harry and Aliona revived their top-scoring quickstep and put together a rock 'n' roll showdance in the Grand Final.

'It was pretty even,' he says. 'Chelsee is a beautiful, very natural dancer and Jason has that ability to entertain, to create an electric atmosphere, and to pull something special out of the bag. I had to bring my A-game.'

He admits he was terrified before the live final, but adds, 'I've never been shy about the fact that I'm competitive.' The pop pin-up gave it his all and triumphed on the night.

'I couldn't believe it had all happened, there was so much to take in,' he recalls. 'I had never experienced such nerves as on final night, and before it started I thought I couldn't cope but, as it was in Blackpool, the home of ballroom dancing, there was a magical atmosphere. When the quickstep started, a wave of relaxation came over me and, for the first time, I genuinely enjoyed dancing. It was an incredible feeling and that was the best dance I've ever done. From then on all I wanted to do was dance.'

After a stint on the tour, Harry went back to the day job, recording with his McFly bandmates but he has fond memories of his dancing days.

'*Strictly* has given me lots of happy memories and a bit more confidence,' he says. 'It's a nice, positive overall experience. The most satisfying thing is meeting members of the public, who tell me they enjoyed watching me dance. It's a special thing to have entertained people.

The McFly drummer was wracked with nerves at the launch show but had already been dubbed 'Champ'.

'*Strictly* fans aren't necessarily going to go out and buy our albums, but if people like me that's great. When it comes to McFly, they're a good bunch of guys and we want to carry on being a band as long as possible.'

One thing in his life has changed since the show. In May, on a well-earned holiday in St Lucia with girlfriend Izzy, Harry popped the question. He now plans to show off his new skills on their big day.

'We shall certainly be dancing at the wedding,' he says. 'There's been a lot to think about so we haven't choreographed a first dance but Izzy's been wanting to get lessons so we'll definitely be doing something, for sure.'

BRUNO TAKES THE FLOOR

There's never a dull moment with Bruno Tonioli around and the last series saw the excitable Italian get steamed up over Harry and Holly, dissolve into giggles over Robbie's hip thrusts and launch himself at fellow judge Alesha. As always, he had a ballroom blast.

'I think this was the best one ever, because of the combination of talent and entertainment value,' he explains. 'It will be a tough act to follow.'

But the optimistic judge is confident that series ten will be every bit as good.

'It keeps getting better,' he says. 'It's like sport. You're always trying to improve on the result of the prior game. It's like the Olympics, but we do it every year!'

What were your thoughts when you saw the series nine line-up?

It was the variety that I liked. We had the young, like Harry, the older, like Lulu and Anita, and the funny, like Russell and Nancy. Then you had the potential winners like Jason and Chelsee. The casting couldn't have been better.

Apart from the finalists, who impressed you?

Holly and Alex were really good. Anita was not one of the best dancers but she was one of the better performers, because her acting skills came in handy. She always made things look right for her, so she was enchanting and great to watch.

Then there's Robbie Savage – the metrosexual blond bombshell. He was absolutely brilliant.

Bruno's Best Bits

Edwina Currie's foxtrot
'That little bit there was like watching a bendy bus negotiating a tight roundabout.'

Anita's salsa
'A tropical tutti frutti cocktail full of flavour and spice.'

Holly's Chicago *tango*
'You got me going. Tantalising behind bars. I want to be a criminal. Everybody will queue up to join you in jail.'

Jason's paso doble
'You tried to make a big meal out of the paso and you got indigestion.'

Chelsee's quickstep
'Chelsee the pocket rocket is off, higher than you could possibly reach.'

Jason's rumba
'I didn't feel anything tonight – it was neither Arthur or Martha!'

Robbie's salsa
'RRRrrrobbie, the salsa, the dance of courtship – you went at it as if it were a primeval fertility rite.'

Nancy's Halloween rumba
'Oh Nancy, emerging from the coffin, looking like the queen of the night, but you dance like the walking dead.'

Harry's Grease *jive*
'Harry, all greased up, leather-clad rippling muscles, action-packed expression of youth. I almost hate you.'

Did you know who was likely to win the final?

No, because they all worked very hard. But I think Harry was the right winner. There was hardly anything between them but he just nailed it. He had never danced before and, out of nowhere, he was just incredible. His showdance was brilliant and his ballroom was superb. Plus he's a great kid and he's good-looking – which always helps.

Most Memorable Moments

Nancy Dell'Olio emerging from the coffin like a zombie. There was a lot of comedy. Russell Grant being fired from a cannon and being shot across Wembley arena was hard to top. And Jason Donovan messing up the jive, when he was he was on course for four tens, is memorable for different reasons.

How was Craig Revel Horwood as head judge?

He fitted into Len's shoes very well. He loves being in charge. It feeds his ego and loves playing the baddie!

Colin SALMON

Colin is best known for his acting but he has a secret musical background which means he's bound to have rhythm. He began his showbiz career as the drummer in a punk band and now plays trumpet with his own jazz quartet in his spare time. When it comes to dancing, Colin is an enthusiastic amateur.

'I love dance and always have loved dance,' he says. 'When I was a kid growing up, and we went to a Caribbean party, the kids danced and we were encouraged. My mum was quite English and I'd go to an English party and get told to stop showing off. If you don't get encouraged as a child to dance, you don't dance, so I would say to all parents if you see your children dancing, encourage them. Some of my earliest happy memories are being at my dad's Jamaican friends' parties.'

London-born Colin is best known for his role as Charles Robinson in three Bond movies - *Die Another Day*, *Tomorrow Never Dies* and *The World Is Not Enough* – alongside Pierce Brosnan and Dame Judi Dench. He first sprang to fame as Detective Sergeant Robert Oswald in classic cop drama *Prime Suspect 2*, with Helen Mirren, and has also starred in the *Resident Evil* movies, *Bad Girls* and two episodes of *Doctor Who*.

Having turned 50 last December, the handsome actor – once named in *People* magazine's poll of 50 Most Beautiful People in the world – decided it was time to let his hair down. 'My wife has been on at me for ages to do it and I wasn't sure,' he admits. 'But I hit a certain age and I decided that it was time to have some fun! Those people I have told are really excited, a lot of people in my life have always been very supportive and this is for them really.'

Being a keen cricketer in his spare time, Colin has heard about the *Strictly* experience from some impressive sources. 'I know three ex-champions - Darren Gough, Mark Ramprakash and Tom Chambers - and they all had a ball, but the only advice they have given me is to look after my feet!'

At 6'4" Colin is likely to cut an imposing figure on the dance floor – but he's not afraid to camp it up when it comes to the costumes. 'I do panto every year and I have to say that I do like dressing up as the dame,' he laughs. 'There you go. I've said it.'

Kristina RIHANNOFF

Kristina made it to the final for the first time in series nine, dancing with actor and singer Jason Donovan. And the Aussie showman will prove a hard act to follow.

'Last year was amazing,' says the sexy Siberian. 'It will be very hard to top the attitude Jason had. We had an amazing chemistry and understanding and a similar attitude towards work. I couldn't have wished for a better partner.'

Facing stiff competition from Harry Judd and Chelsee Healey, Jason pulled off a perfect score for his showdance and bagged 38 for his Priscilla tango, finishing top after two dances. But Kristina was not surprised they came third.

'I knew Harry was going to win because he's a young boy in a very popular band and there were tons of girls screaming their heads off,' she says. 'But it wasn't about winning with Jason, I wanted to bring the best out of him and to me he was the best actor and performer.'

Kristina was born in Siberia and began to study ballet at the age of six. She went on to train in Latin and standard styles, as well as rhythm and theatre arts. She entered her first competition at 7 years old and began teaching dance at 16.

Five years later she achieved a Master's degree in Tourism and Hospitality. In 2001, she moved to Seattle and three years later she represented the US at the World Exhibition in Blackpool. After finding a new partner in Michael Wentink, she won the South African Latin championships and, in 2007, was a semi-finalist in the British Open.

Kristina was thrown in the deep end when she joined *Strictly* in series six, and was paired with John Sergeant, whose comic antics on the dance floor had viewers voting for him again and again. The following year, she teamed up with boxer Joe Calzaghe, who won her heart, if not the judges' scores. They were knocked out in week five, but Kristina says, 'I feel like a winner – I'm in a beautiful relationship that I really treasure.'

For the next series, the blonde bombshell is hoping for another natural performer. 'I would love to have someone as dedicated as Jason. He trusted me 100 per cent and if you don't have trust then you can't go very far. I'd like somebody from movies, film, theatre, because they are very comfortable with the performance.

'It's an entertainment show as much as a dance show.'

Dani HARMER

Dani has been a familiar face on children's TV since she landed the lead role in *The Story of Tracy Beaker* in 2002. She went on to play the character for ten years and also star in her own show, *Dani's House*. Earlier this year she took part in *Let's Dance For Sport Relief*, and she thinks the experience has given her a insight into the *Strictly* experience.

'It will definitely help,' says Dani. '*Let's Dance For Sport Relief* is like the perfect warm up to *Strictly*. I know what it feels like to have to learn a routine in a short space of time, and I know what it feels like to have to dance in front of millions of people. That will help, but I'm still incredibly nervous about stepping onto the ballroom floor.'

As nervous as she is, Dani enjoyed the launch show and says she couldn't believe she had actually made it to hallowed *Strictly* floor. 'I love the show so it's a dream come true,' she says. 'As soon as we walked in to the studio Richard Arnold and I both let out a scream. It suddenly felt really real. But I'm slowly calming

down now that I know we've only got a few weeks to learn the dances.'

The 23-year-old did a little bit of dance at stage school but the ballroom is a new experience for her. However she admits it was a fleet-footed movie icon that made her want to act. 'If I could dance with anyone it would be Gene Kelly because I was brought up watching all of his films,' she reveals. '*Singing in the Rain* was what inspired me to be in this industry.'

Now Dani has a new dancing hero to look up to – partner and tango king Vincent Simone. 'I'm over the moon to get Vincent,' she beams. 'He was my first choice so I got what I wanted. I've always wanted to learn how to tango, and now I might get the chance!'

A committed tomboy, the CBBC star is happy to embrace the ultra-girly wardrobe of ballroom. 'I wouldn't say I'm overly excited about the spray tan but I will embrace it and enjoy it. As for the sequins and glitter – I'm a girl, I can't wait!'

Vincent
SIMONE

Last season, Vincent was paired with politician Edwina Currie. But her cha-cha-cha and foxtrot curried no favours with the judges and the unfortunate pair were out in the first elimination.

'The main problem with Edwina Currie was that she wasn't bad enough and she wasn't good enough,' reasons Vincent. 'In this show, it's important that you either use the fun aspects of the dancing like we've seen with Ann Widdecombe and Russell Grant, or you get someone who can learn and make it all the way to the top. Edwina was sort of in between. She had a bit of rhythm, she could move, so it was a tricky one. Maybe people wanted another Ann Widdecombe but you can't follow her.'

It wasn't the first time the Italian charmer was knocked out early – as the same fate awaited him with Stephanie Beacham in series five. 'A real lady, but scary,' laughs Vincent. 'I'm not scared of any woman now after dancing with her.'

He had better luck with his first celebrity, Louisa Lytton, who took him to the quarter finals and his series six partner, Rachel Stevens, who came second. 'It's been up and down but it's the same for all of us. You can't get good partners every year.'

Vincent was born in Foggia, near Naples, and showed a talent for dancing at a young age. When he was seven, he and his parents enrolled in a dance school 'It was a real family affair,' he says. 'We all started learning to dance together and we loved it.' The tutor soon recognised his talent and he and his partner entered their first competition in Rome at the age of nine, coming first out of seventy couples. He was Juvenile Italian Champion at 10 and, with a different partner, regained the title at 12, 13, 14 and 15 years old. At 17, he moved to England and met Flavia. They have been professional partners for 13 years.

When he's not dancing, Vincent is a devoted dad to three-year-old Luca. 'After a day of training, working hard, I'm tired and I get back home and see my little sausage – which is what I call him – and he puts a smile on my face,' says the proud parent. 'He makes me laugh, I play with him. All the other dancers can go home and put their feet up on the sofa, but I can't do that because I'm a dad. But it's good. It makes me very happy.'

CRAIG
CALLS
THE
SHOTS

Craig Revel Horwood is always looking for hip action in the Latin dances, but he got more than he bargained for in the last series – when Robbie Savage jumped on the judges' desk and aimed a few thrusts in his direction. The Aussie judge was not impressed. 'That's the sort of moment one really doesn't need as a judge,' he says. 'It may have been entertaining but it doesn't belong in the ballroom. I can't condone it – but I'm sure it won him a few extra votes.' He was more taken with the dancing skills of three finalists. Here's his take on last series.

Did Harry deserve to win?

Definitely. Harry was immaculate in every way and that's because he worked hard and had a passion for it. His quickstep was phenomenal and deserved every single 10 that it got. Plus he's cute, has an adorable personality, and he's a teenage heart-throb. The whole package.

What did you think of the runners up?

I loved Chelsee although she could have been a little more out there. But she had great rhythm and a great sense of the dance. Jason is an extremely hard worker. He beats himself up a lot over the dance, because he is not a natural talent so he will practise over and over until his body gets it, then he entertains and performs. That's why he trains so much. But it's the result that matters and what he achieved was fantastic.

Who was the biggest surprise?

Lulu. When she sings, she sings in time and she's rhythmical and fantastic but that didn't translate into her body and her feet. I thought she'd come out and nail it!

Who went too soon?

Dan Lobb could have done better. He's tall, he's handsome, he had everything going for him physically, but he didn't apply himself. He was rhythmically challenged but if he had buckled down he could have been in longer. I felt sorry for Rory because he had talent, he loved the show, loved dancing and had a great rapport with Erin but the audience didn't vote.

Who was the worst?

Nancy was the worst, but the funniest with it. She is the most self-deluded person I've ever met. She listened to criticism and said, 'Thank you, darling. I was fabulous, wasn't I?' It was like water off a duck's back and she really thought she was amazing. It was quite frightening.

Who was the most entertaining?

Russell Grant always provided more entertainment than dancing skill. He used his personality to his best advantage and he was loved by the nation. In the Latin dances he had good funk and disco, an enormous amount of energy, and the right mindset. When he went blank he made stuff up. He exuded sparkle.

Are you looking forward to having Darcey on the panel?

Very much so. Darcey has devoted her life to dance and she is someone who trained eight hours a day en pointe as a Prima Ballerina. There are not many people who can do that in the world. The professionals look up to her and we're extremely fortunate to have her.

Craig's Comments

Dan's salsa
'Lumpustuous.'

Rory's salsa
'It was like a rat caught on a sticky strip.'

Anita's salsa
'I thought it was a bit like Bonny Langford being chased by a barking Dalmation.'

Chelsee's flight attendant quickstep.
'Two words – First Class!'

Russell's foxtrot
'I would advise a more masculine approach for this dance. A little less Barbara and a little more Rambo.'

On Jason's showdance
'Ferocious and full on, darling. Get that woman a restraining order.'

Alex's Halloween paso doble
'I quite like the idea of Dracula chasing innocent virgin blood and I think you played that extremely well. I almost found it erotic. That probably says a lot more about me than you.'

Nancy's Halloween rumba
'Dance horribilus. The moment you stepped out of the sarcophagus, darling, is the moment it all went horribly wrong.'

It takes TWO

There have been some perfect partners on past series, but this year the show has a brand-new double act behind the scenes as well. Executive producers Andrea Hamilton and Glenn Coomber have joined forces at the *Strictly* helm and are 'absolutely overwhelmed' to be part of the glitziest show on TV. 'We've said from the very beginning that it's a "pinch yourself" feeling,' admits Glenn. 'This show is all those clichés – a national treasure, the jewel in the crown of the BBC schedule – and they've given it to us. It's lovely. It had such a good year last year that it's a real honour to be able to cover it and look after it.'

Although they have never worked together before the pair share a wealth of TV experience, and much of it dance-related. Andrea worked on *So You Think You Can Dance* before becoming series editor on *The Voice* and Glenn has worked on *Fame Academy* and *I'm a Celebrity... Get Me Out of Here* as well as being executive producer of ITV's *Dancing on Ice* for the last two years.

'We come from different but similar backgrounds and it's quite a good complement of experience and ideas and its working very well,' says Glenn. 'It's like we were plucked out of an exec talent contest and formed our own boy–girl band.'

Andrea and Glenn think that series ten will be 'even more brilliant and fabulous' than last year's, above and opposite

'We get on really well and it's working out fine,' confirms Andrea. 'Three and a half months in and we haven't shouted at each other once.'

Glenn has already worked with resident joker Anton du Beke on *Hole in the Wall* so at least he's ready for the constant gags. The other regulars have welcomed the pair with open arms. 'There's no feeling of "Oh you're new, we've been doing it for years,"' says Andrea. 'It's good when fresh energy comes in and I feel very welcome here.'

The runaway success of the previous series might seem daunting to the two new producers, but Andrea insists that this 'national treasure' still has plenty of sparkle left to give.

'I don't feel like anything has ever got to its pinnacle,' she says. 'This has got all the right ingredients to go on for years and I don't see why its tenth series couldn't be better than the year before. It's an amazing show which we're pushing to become even more brilliant and fabulous than before.'

Johnny BALL

Johnny Ball is following in the dainty footsteps of daughter Zoe, a former contestant and the current presenter of *It Takes Two*. With a host of perfect 10s under her belt, and coming third in series three, she is a hard act to follow. But the hardest thing for the devoted dad was keeping it from her.

'I kept it secret from Zoe for six weeks, which I hated doing because we tell each other everything,' he explains. 'But they asked me to keep it quiet from Zoe because they wanted a camera there when she was told, so she only heard the day before one of the papers wrote that I was in. But she's over the moon. She's absolutely thrilled about it, as are my five grandchildren. I know that on *It Takes Two* she'll be as impartial as possible for a girl who loves her dad. For me, the great worry is causing her embarrassment.'

The TV legend was born in Bristol and later moved to Bolton, Lancashire. After school he joined the RAF before becoming a Butlin's redcoat and club entertainer. Throughout the 1970s and '80s Johnny was a regular face on children's TV, renowned for putting the fun into maths and science programmes with his unique and eccentric style. Famous shows included *Think of a Number, Think Again* and *Think Backwards*.

Now 74, Johnny is the oldest contestant ever to grace the *Strictly* dance floor. 'Thank God they've asked me now,' he jokes. 'Imagine if they'd waited another 20 years!'

Johnny was on holiday in the Algarve when he was approached about the show and says that, after a couple of celebratory drinks with wife Di, he threw himself into preparations. 'I started getting fit straight away and I'm already much fitter than I was,' he reveals. 'I've never trained in my life so I started training for this and I'm so glad I've done it, because I feel fitter immediately, which is tremendous.'

With current champ Aliona and former finalist Zoe on his side, Johnny has all the support he needs to take on the ballroom. And having taught a whole generation of kids to enjoy maths, he won't have any trouble counting the steps.

Aliona VILANI

It was third time lucky for Aliona Vilani as she scooped the trophy with Harry Judd. Her first *Strictly* outing ended in week three and her second saw her reach the final with Matt Baker and lose out to Kara Tointon. But the McFly star managed to drum up the glittering prize.

'It felt amazing and very rewarding,' smiles Aliona. 'Knowing the British public were behind us and voted for us was wonderful.'

While the nation was falling for Harry, the ever-professional Aliona seemed immune to his charms. 'I always thought of him as a cute sloth, which I kept calling him. He was like a younger brother to me. I know it didn't look like that on screen but that's my job.'

The Russian redhead got her first taste of dance training at a school for classical ballet and performing arts. At 13, she was invited to train at the Kaiser Dance Academy in New York, where she learned salsa, hip hop and jazz and three years later she became a US National Champion in 10-Dance in the Youth category.

After representing the States in an international competition and winning the Amateur Ballroom category, she became the youngest professional dancer in America, at 17.

In 2006, Aliona moved to Los Angeles to teach, perform and compete. Having bagged the biggest bauble of all it was there she headed for a well-earned rest.

'You have such a great time together, when it ends it feels weird not to see each other every day,' she admits. 'But it's such a tough process that when it's over you feel "OK, I want some rest." You just want a bit of your life back and to see friends and family.'

After being crowned champ, Aliona has a lot to live up to in series ten, but she only asks one thing from her celeb – a lot of hard work.

'Matt and Harry weren't brilliant dancers when I started with them but they both worked really hard,' she says. 'I told Harry he could work as much as he wanted to work, I could do 9 or 13 hours a day. He went for it and that's why it worked.'

Another stab at the final wouldn't go amiss either. 'To get to the final again would be amazing,' she says. 'It's such an honour to do the show and I love my job, I love dancing every day. To be in the final means that people love what you do and that means everything.'

Denise VAN OUTEN

Blonde bombshell Denise is thrilled to be partnered with James Jordan – for all the right reasons. 'I'm so happy I've got him,' she says. 'One because I think he's brilliant and two because he lives really close to me, so I won't have to travel far.'

Although she now lives in Kent, Denise was born and bred in Essex and showed a flair for performance from an early age. Having enrolled in the Sylvia Young Theatre School she played Eponine in *Les Miserables* at the age of twelve and also appeared in the Anthony Newley production of *Stop the World I Want to Get Off*. In 1997, she landed her big television break as presenter on *The Big Breakfast*. She went on to star in various West End productions including *Chicago* and *Legally Blonde – The Musical*. In 2007, she met Lee Mead while judging on BBC talent show *Any Dream Will Do*. He won the show, and Denise's heart, and they were wed in April 2009. They now have a two-year-old daughter, Betsy.

Although no stranger to musicals, Denise is unsure her West End experience will help in her quest for the glitterball. 'It will help the performance, in the same way it will help other people here who act because you take on a different persona with the different dances,' she muses. 'But the dancing here is completely different. I've only ever done one show that I've danced in, and that's Chicago, which was 11 years ago so it's all new to me.'

Coincidentally, it was the memory of that show that tempted her to sign up to *Strictly*. 'Most years I've tried to watch, but often been in shows, so I've never been able to do it myself,' she explains. 'Last year I was in *Legally Blonde*, and I remember being sat in my dressing room watching Holly Valance doing her *Chicago* number, and I just thought "I want to be doing that!" I knew that when the chance came that I really wanted to do it, and this year finally I can!'

The 38-year-old star is looking forward to training and getting fit in the process of the show. 'When I was a kid I just loved to dance, and I can't wait to just get into it, and be feeling really fit and healthy. I'm really looking forward to the group numbers the most, all dancing together and having a laugh.'

James JORDAN

He may unleash his fiery temper on the judges but last year saw James reduced to tears – by sweet little Alex Jones.

'At the start, I was concerned because she is young and beautiful and everyone expects the young and beautiful to be able to dance,' he explains. 'Then we got in the studio and started working on things and it was like "Oh dear, I've got bambi!" I remember going home on the third day and actually crying!

'But she worked so hard, and we had such a great relationship and she really improved every week. I've enjoyed all my series of *Strictly* but last year I had such a great time. Going in and teaching Alex every day was a joy.'

James grew up in Kent, the son of former dance teachers who tutored the famous Peggy Spencer formation team: regular contributors to *Come Dancing*. James reluctantly agreed to dance classes at 11, but soon found he had talent. After six years on the youth circuit, he was ranked one of the best in the world but, at 21, James took a six-month break before travelling to Poland for a try-out with Ola. They proved the perfect match and waltzed down the aisle in 2003.

The talented couple joined *Strictly* in series four and James quickly gained a reputation as a harsh teacher.

'I do have a short temper – I'm not going to deny that – but when it comes to teaching I'm probably one of the most patient because I have never been a natural dancer. I don't profess to be a gifted dancer, but I'm a great teacher.

'I will never get angry with someone who is giving it 100 per cent. As soon as I feel someone is not giving me everything, I will get frustrated because they only get one shot and I don't want them to waste it.'

The glittering prize still eludes James, but he has a constant reminder of his goal at home.

'Ola has a glitterball sitting at home on her bedside cabinet,' he explains. 'I see it every morning when I wake up and sometimes she winds me up because she moves it to my side, so when I go to bed it's just sitting there. But really, I was very proud of her.

'I would never be competitive against my wife. When it comes to Ola, I'm happier for her to win than me.'

Len's
LOWDOWN

LEN GOODMAN has been shining up his shoes and digging out his dickie bow in preparation for the tenth series of *Strictly* and has seen the show go from strength to strength.

'I honestly didn't think we'd make it past series one,' he recalls. 'I remember thinking, "No one's interested in ballroom dancing." I didn't think there was much future for it. Now we're at series ten and I would hate to be one of the producers, because to come up with something that can beat series nine is going to be a terrifically hard job.'

The London-born head judge was impressed with the celebrity dancers in series nine and feels it was the best series ever.

'It was a marvellous year and the last three were fabulous,' he says. 'Harry was a worthy winner. Sometimes, in previous years, I have felt that the best dancer hasn't won, but this time he really did.

'It was the most intriguing bunch – Audley Harrison, huge guy with size 17 feet, Russell Grant, little chubby chap, then you had Nancy… Anton did a wonderful job with her. And Edwina. Even though she was the first to go she wasn't that bad. Dan could have gone instead, or Audley or Russell. That was what was lovely about this year – there was a little group and you didn't know which of them would go and then there was the top group, any one of which could win. By the time we got to the last five, it could have been Alex , Holly, Jason, Chelsee or Harry.'

Was Nancy a Surprise?

No, I always had a feeling she wouldn't be lighting up the ballroom! But that's one of the joys of *Strictly*. I wouldn't like it so much, and I don't think the viewers would either, if everyone was terrific. It is TV entertainment so you want to see those that are not much good and you can laugh along with.

Looking forward to having Darcey as a judge?

Obviously I was sad that Alesha was leaving, but you can't get anyone with better credentials than Darcey Bussell. One of the great prima ballerinas of all time so I'm sure she will be an asset to the panel. I think the secret to the judging panel is that you get a balanced critique. My experience is in ballroom and Latin dancing so I look at technique, Bruno looks at the passion and performance level, Craig loves the story of the dance and the connection between the couple, and then we have Darcey who will be looking at the artistry and lyricism.

Shock exit?

I was very disappointed when Rory went. I didn't think he deserved to be third to go. OK, there were others that were better but there were some, like Nancy and Russell, who were a lot worse.

Favourite moments of the series?

Robbie Savage jumping up on the judges' desk and thrusting himself at Craig's face was wonderful. The look of shock-horror on Craig's face was hilarious. But it was Russell who gave us the most memorable moment of the series. Long after we've forgotten about Harry Judd and Chelsee Healey, we'll remember Russell Grant being fired out of a cannon. For me, it was a truly iconic *Strictly* moment.

Could you pick the winner at the beginning of the final?

No. It could have been any one of them. I think Jason was a tad unlucky not to have been in the final two. As much as Chelsee was terrific, Jason was such a great dancer and he embraced the show, totally. But he started incredibly strong and sometimes that's not the best way to go. People like to see you struggle and overcome. I knew Harry was pretty good but he also improved a lot, especially in ballroom, and he did a terrific showdance number. Of the three showdance numbers I thought Chelsee's was the weakest, because it was more disco.

Who else stood out?

Anita made a great impression and went on to do the tour. What I loved about Anita was her professionalism. Whatever she does, she does it 100 per cent and she loved every minute. She was full of joy. Lulu did really well. You're always a bit concerned for someone in their sixties. You wonder whether their energy levels will stay up. And as you get older you can't remember things quite so well!

Who surprised you?

I never expected Robbie Savage to be any good, especially after week one when Craig gave him a two. He was absolutely mortified. He was virtually in tears and on the verge of quitting. But he knuckled down and that's one of the keys to the sportsmen. They get beaten down, they have a bad game, but they come back with that will to win. He's the best footballer we've had by miles because most of them are terrible.

How did Craig do as head judge on your one week off?

I couldn't think of a better person to be head judge than Craig Revel Horwood. He knows what he's talking about and he tells it as it is. He's far braver than I. One of my weaknesses is that I admire all the celebrities for their pluck. So as much as I may criticise the dancing, I never forget that you've got to have nerves to come out and dance live in front of 10 million people in a genre that is totally out of your comfort zone. I wouldn't do it!

What was the Wembley show like?

It was wonderful. What a show and what an atmosphere! In the studio, if Craig says something nasty, 300 people boo. At Wembley, 5,000 boo. It was the bee's knees.

Over all nine series who is the best winner?

Alesha is the best female winner, and Harry is the best male. That's my feeling. Alesha had such fluidity of movement and she was equally at home in ballroom as she was in Latin. One of the best dances I've ever seen is her Viennese waltz. It was fantastic. She really was a terrific dancer.

Best person who didn't win?

Ricky Whittle. He was great, very good. I'm not knocking Chris Hollins because I really like him. But if I'm brutally frank Ricky should have won it. His ballroom was fantastic, he was such a good dancer.

How has *Strictly* changed over the years?

I always think of shows like a plant. You get a young plant and you stick it in a pot and you see how it grows. Every now and then you give it a little bit of pruning – but you never pull it up and chop off the roots. You nurture it, and feed it and prune it and watch it develop. That's what's happened to *Strictly*. It started off as a willowy little plant, and over nine series we've seen it slightly pruned, we've had different gardeners come in to help it along, and it's grown and bloomed and blossomed.

Len's Best Comments

Chelsee's salsa
'When I got here I was a little bit chilly round the willy but that warmed me up a treat.'

Lulu's cha-cha-cha
'There was plenty of "Boom-Bang-a-Bang" but nothing to "Shout" about.'

Audley's salsa
'Everything was orderly, Audley.'

Holly's salsa
'You flew through Artem's legs and then he flew through yours. He was like a mechanic checking for an oil leak.'

Jason's tango
'I'm going to call you the midwife 'cause you keep delivering.'

Rory's cha-cha-cha
'You're like the government. There's a lot going on and not all of it's good.'

Harry's waltz
'More rise and fall than Jordan jogging.'

Russell's American smooth to 'I Am What I Am'
'I am what I am, you are what you are, and that was what that was.'

On Nancy's rumba
'The dance of love – and there were moments of Mills and Boon and moments of meals on wheels.'

Strictly CROSSWORD

ACROSS

6. Robbie ___, footballer who broke his nose on the *Strictly* dance floor performing a knee slide towards the camera **(6)**

7. Dancer whose regular professional partner is 11A **(4,4)**

9. Nicholas ___, newsreader who fell at the first in 2006 **(4)**

10. Natalie ___, Aussie dancer who was knocked out with Audley Harrison in week six **(4)**

11. Ballroom specialist and *Strictly* ever-present who's yet to reach the semis **(5)**

12. ___ Phillips, former GMTV presenter who failed to wow the judges despite the efforts of Brendan Cole **(5)**

13. Judge who saves his harshest comments for his colleague seated to his right **(3)**

14. Children In ___, fundraiser in which Ola and 19A beat 1D and Rochelle Wiseman in 2010 **(4)**

16. *Strictly* presenter who partnered 11A for the charity at 14A in 2008 **(4)**

18. ___ Lobb, *Daybreak* presenter who was the second celeb to leave in 2011 **(3)**

19. ___ Judd, pop drummer who averaged an impressive 35.6 points on his way to victory in 2011 **(5)**

24. Darren ___, cricketer who in 2005 became the first male celebrity to win the competition **(5)**

25. ___ Bunton, singer who spiced up her life when she finished third with 8D in 2006 **(4)**

26. Sequence of movements of the feet that makes up a dance **(4)**

27 Nancy ___, celeb who was told by Craig on Halloween week that she'd have been better off staying in the coffin **(8)**

28 Russian dancer who partnered 19A to victory **(6)**

DOWN

1. Professional dancer who partnered 22D **(3,5)**

2. Large weapon that turned Russell Grant into a shooting star **(6)**

3. Craig ___, actor who was eliminated in front of his home crowd at the Tower Ballroom in Blackpool in 2009 **(5)**

4. Russian dancer who took Holly Valance to the semi-final in 2011 **(5)**

5. ___ Donovan, Aussie star who went one stage further and made the final **(5)**

8. Darren ___, dancer who's real-life partner, both on and off the dance floor, is Lilia **(7)**

15. Matt ___, former EastEnder who finished runner-up with Flavia behind Alesha in 2007 **(2,6)**

17. John ___, political reporter who pulled out of 2008's contest as winning would have been "a joke too far" **(8)**

20. ___ Healey, rugby player who made it as far as week 12 in 2008 with 7A **(6)**

21. Alex ___, semi-finalist who hosts *Let's Dance For Sport Relief* **(5)**

22. Denise ___, Olympic gold medallist who got silver in *Strictly* dancing with 1D **(5)**

23. ___ Manners, actress who teamed up with Brendan in the second series **(5)**

Find all the winners hidden in the wordsearch grid. See if you can pair them all up and work out in which order they won *Strictly Come Dancing*.

```
T T E N N E B N E R R A D N V D Y
M D D U J Y R R A H N S D J E K I
K A R A T O I N T O N F I G S P Y
R N R A R G T S M I N L A N T L K
N E A K D R N R L I L M I K N I I
S D L A R J E L R H R L Y A I L N
R B U T D A O N A H P C L R V I A
E M R L U H M L G A A E I E G A L
B E J E S C F P K O S K A N I K I
M P T I N P W A R H U K I H H O V
A I R N E D H E A A S G L A C P A
H H Y N V S A D H A K A H R M Y N
C C N T A A I N I T C A A D E L O
M Y L T D X L T C S T H S Y T O I
O L A J O R D A N O H A A H R V L
T N T N A R B N O T L E M S A A A
C A M I L L A D A L L E R U P H N
```

CELEBS

ALESHA DIXON
CHRIS HOLLINS
DARREN GOUGH
HARRY JUDD
JILL HALFPENNY
KARA TOINTON
MARK RAMPRAKASH
NATASHA KAPLINSKY
TOM CHAMBERS

DANCERS

ALIONA VILANI
ARTEM CHIGVINTSEV
BRENDAN COLE
CAMILLA DALLERUP
DARREN BENNETT
KAREN HARDY
LILIA KOPYLOVA
MATTHEW CUTLER
OLA JORDAN

	CELEB	DANCER
SCD1	_____	& _____
SCD2	_____	& _____
SCD3	_____	& _____
SCD4	_____	& _____
SCD5	_____	& _____
SCD6	_____	& _____
SCD7	_____	& _____
SCD8	_____	& _____
SCD9	_____	& _____

Louis SMITH

After powering to a silver medal on the pommel horse at the London 2012 Olympics, gymnast Louis Smith won't have any trouble lifting partner Flavia in the dances. And after performing to an expectant crowd of millions, he is ready to handle any pressure *Strictly* can throw at him.

'This is very different,' he says. 'For the Olympics I trained 19 years for that opportunity and got one chance to prove what all those 19 years were worth so it was incredibly nerve-wracking. Whereas with this, we're straight into dancing, having fun, you do your routine the crowd are standing up and clapping, so it's completely different and more fun.'

The Peterborough-born athlete started training at seven and in his teens he was two-time European Youth Champion on the pommel horse. In 2008, at the age of 19, he won a bronze medal at the Beijing Olympics and in 2012 he scooped the silver, as well as a bronze for the team event.

Signing up to the show means the 23-year-old has avoided the post-Olympic deflation. 'Coming off the back of the Olympics and having been on such a high, I think this is one of the only shows that can match that in terms of the adrenalin buzz and being part of something special,' he admits.

For now, however, he has had to ditch gymnastic training to concentrate on the dancing. 'I think it's impossible to train for gymnastics and train for this at the same time. I think it's going to be very full-on in terms of getting ready for the individual dances. If I go on until Christmas that's four or five months out but my coach is happy. He messaged me to say "Have a wicked time on *Strictly*, do your best, hope it all goes well." But he's definitely expecting me back in the gym afterwards.'

The lithe, athletic Olympian is sure to be pulling some spectacular tricks on the dance floor but after an impressive flip on the launch show, he's keeping it under wraps. 'The group dance was just a little taste,' he says. 'I let you try the dessert but you can't have it until the end of the meal now.'

Being a gymnast is sure to help Louis with jazzing up the routine but it also helps in another department – wardrobe. 'I wear a leotard for my day job,' he jokes. 'The lycra and sequins don't faze me. Bring it on!'

Flavia
CACACE

Before the last series Flavia said she hoped for 'a partner who is enthusiastic and willing to win'. That wish upon a star sent her astrologist Russell Grant – who couldn't have been more enthusiastic if he tried.

'Russell made it so effortless because he was easy to work with and so much fun,' she recalls. 'And so much enthusiasm! You never know who you are going to get for a partner but you just hope that they are enthusiastic. Russell and Anita are the perfect examples of the mood that people should come into the show with.'

The inventive Italian soon had the stargazer mounting mechanical bulls, snoozing on stage with his teddy bear and even being fired out of a cannon – and the audience loved it, keeping them in until week eight.

'I'll miss him this year,' says Flavia. 'I speak to him every week and he'll definitely be watching.'

Flavia was born in Naples, the youngest of six children, but her family moved to Guildford when she was four. Failing to find a ballet class for her daughter, Flavia's mum enrolled her in a ballroom class when she was six and she was instantly hooked. At 12 she began competing and at 16 she was asked to try out with a young Italian who was visiting her dance school – and her long-term partnership with Vincent Simone was born.

The tango supremoes joined the show in series four and since then there have been many ups and downs, including a week one exit with Phil Daniels and making the final with Matt di Angelo. But her fondest *Strictly* memories are still with Vincent.

'My favourite moments are probably when I do the solo numbers with Vincent, because that's when you are dancing at your best. You can never push yourself to the limit unless you are dancing with a professional dance partner.'

While the last series was all about fun, this series, Flavia hopes, will be about winning. 'Last year I took it on as a totally different competition,' she reveals. 'I wanted to put on a good show for the audience and I wanted Russell to enjoy it, but I never felt we were going to win. It would be nice to feel, this time, that I had the potential to go all the way as far as the ability of the celebrity dancing is concerned. I haven't had that for a while.'

Fern BRITTON

Fern Britton has already had a taste of the *Strictly* experience, dancing the jive in the 2010 Christmas Special. Len compared her to a trifle – 'Fruity on top, a bit spongy below' – but Fern had the dancing bug. 'The small taste of training I had two years ago really excited me,' says the presenter. 'I am ready to learn something new in life.' She admits she loved dancing with Matthew Cutler so much she was upset when it was all over. 'We did it for three weeks and when it was over, I was bereft, beside myself. I actually did cry in the kitchen. I was quite sad.'

Fern, the daughter of beloved English actor Tony Britton, was born in London and raised in Buckinghamshire. She began her TV career as a continuity announcer and newsreader on a local TV station in Plymouth before moving to BBC regional TV and on to BBC1. She presented a multitude of programmes, including *Coast to Coast*, *BBC Breakfast Time* and *GMTV* before teaming up with Philip Schofield to host *This Morning* for ten years, from 1999.

Fern was delighted to be teamed up with former champ Artem – although it was something of a shock. 'I'm really surprised because in the group rehearsals we danced together once for 15 seconds, so we haven't really spent much time together,' she says. 'But I think I got the best, and I wasn't expecting that, so thank you, *Strictly*.'

The much-loved 55-year-old, who is married to TV chef Phil Vickery and has four children, is looking forward to being glammed up on the show. 'I am absolutely ready to get on the production line of *Strictly*,' she laughs. 'Rather like a car factory I shall arrive as an unformed blob shoved onto the conveyor belt. I shall be sprayed, spangled, totally upholstered and polished ready for the showroom! I cannot wait.'

While she's embracing the experience, Fern has a shrewd eye on the competition. 'Absolutely all of the other contestants are impossibly gorgeous and slinky-hipped,' she says. 'Jerry Hall is a complete icon, Victoria Pendleton is a powerhouse, Nicky Byrne and Louis Smith are absolutely adorable. It is going to be a great fun series. Bring it on!'

Artem CHIGVINTSEV

Coming into series nine as reigning champ, Artem was paired with actress and singer Holly Valance – and the heat was on.

'Coming first in my first season, nothing could beat that,' he says. 'In the second season, there was so much pressure and expectations were so high, but I think Holly did brilliantly.'

The fact that the Australian pop star began as one of the bookies' favourites didn't help the Saturday night nerves.

'People think that if you do music videos it's an advantage,' says Artem. 'But when you make a video there are so many cameras shooting you from the best angle possible, so what you see is a combination of different pieces put together, the best of the best. Unfortunately when you do a live show, there's no such thing as starting over so whatever you do that's the dance they're going to judge.

'Plus there are the nerves, even for us. I've done two seasons and performing live is still like dancing for the first time. It never gets easier.'

Artem left his native Russia at 15 to pursue a dance career in Germany, and also trained in the UK and Italy before settling in Los Angeles. After reaching the final of *So You Think You Can Dance*, he performed in shows in Broadway and the West End as well as working as a choreographer.

Joining *Strictly* in series eight, he and partner Kara Tointon won the glitterball as well as each other's hearts. The romantic duo have recently danced together again, along with Robin and Kristina on the *Strictly Presents: Dance To The Music* tour.

For the moment, though, Artem will concentrate on coming up with ideas to wow the *Strictly* audience, like Holly's *Black Swan* dance last year, 'It's always great to do theme dances because you can put a bit more into it. If it's just a dance it's difficult to create something special. When the costume idea, the music and the steps and everything comes together, it feels pretty special.'

But Artem's celebrity pupil will have to be prepared for some harsh treatment in the training room. 'I don't know how Holly wasn't mad at me all the time because I'm a hard teacher,' he admits. 'I always want to get the best out of them and I'm quite strict. I don't give compliments easily. I would be tempted to walk out if I was her!'

Natalie
LOWE

Natalie came tantalisingly close to the glitterball trophy on her first two *Strictly* outings, reaching second place with Ricky Whittle in series seven, and fourth with Scott Maslen the following year. In series nine, she was partnered with Audley Harrison, and training didn't get off to the best of starts.

'He was bookies' favourite to go out first week – but I'm not gonna let that happen!'

In fact, the Australian blonde kept the heavyweight boxer on his toes until week seven and, despite his 6'8" frame and size 17 shoes, she loved dancing with Audley.

'I like a tall boy,' she confesses. 'The last couple of years I've had guys about my own height so when I get in heels I'm a little bit taller. I actually felt really graceful in Audley's arms because he's so much bigger than me.'

Natalie was born in Sydney and, from an early age, watched older brother Glenn and sister Kylie ballroom dancing. At three, she began learning herself and was representing her country at the age of eight. Together with partner Jonathon Doone, she won numerous major under 11s championships and, after a brief stint competing at junior level, she teamed up with Glenn, who was five years older, in the adult category. Natalie appeared in five seasons of *Dancing With The Stars* before moving to the UK show.

Her debut, with Ricky Whittle, saw them pipped at the final post by Chris Hollins, despite higher scores from the judges.

'I was very fresh,' recalls Natalie. 'I was new blood that year. I do think about that moment and think "What could I have done differently?" But it is often about the personality you get and Chris was a lovely guy, like the average Joe, and people love that.'

The willowy blonde went on to the series eight semis with Scott Maslen and says she would love to have another stab at the title with him. 'My three most memorable moments over the series have been the "Hit the Road Jack" jive with Scott, the Viennese on Halloween and our *Jungle Book* quickstep.

'I would love to dance with Scott again and for him not to have such a crazy schedule with *EastEnders*. I think he had the potential to win it. From the get-go he was just naturally beautiful to dance with. I don't know what it was, but he was just great.'

Jerry HALL

The willowy Texan is the second Rolling Stones' ex to grace the *Strictly* floor after bubbly Jo Wood captivated Brendan in series six, but fared less well with the judges. But this Honky-Tonk Woman has been taking plenty of advice from former contestants.

'I've spoken to some friends who have appeared on the show in the past, and they've all said what great fun the whole thing is, totally engrossing,' she says. 'And VERY hard work!'

Jerry was born and raised near Dallas and moved to France where she was discovered by a modelling agent while sunbathing in St Tropez. After moving to Paris to launch a catwalk career, she featured on the cover of a Roxy Music LP and was soon engaged to lead singer Bryan Ferry. In 1977, she met rock legend Mick Jagger and began a 22-year relationship with him that resulted in four children. She later became an actress, starring in the stage version of *The Graduate* and Tim Burton's *Batman*.

Although her six-foot frame proved a boon in the modelling world, her height proved a dance disadvantage when she was growing up. 'As the youngest and tallest of five girls, back in Texas, I always had to take the lead and be the guy, so being led around the ballroom will be a nice experience for me,' she says.

The blonde bombshell couldn't wait to get into the training room to learn the dances – but says it was tough at the start.

'I'm loving it,' she says. 'The first day every muscle in my body was aching but I felt sort of like the penguin in *Happy Feet*, all happy. I think the endorphins are quite good for your brain.'

The 56-year-old blonde will enjoy the themed night as she loves a fancy dress costume – and we might see a historical bent coming into play. 'I like being famous people from history,' says Jerry. 'I've dressed as Marie Antoinette and Cleopatra.'

Even without the robes of Royals, the former model is planning to add a lot of sparkle to the show. 'I'm looking forward to learning all those wonderful dances – the waltz, the American smooth, and especially the tango - it's such a sexy dance, so passionate,' she says. 'And I look forward to hitting the dance floor and cutting the rug, covered from head to toe in diamonds.'

Anton
DU BEKE

Anton's series nine partner, Nancy Dell'Olio, was not famed for her technical prowess on the dance floor but to the chivalrous ballroom supremo, she was 'perfect'.

'Nancy was gorgeous,' he insists. 'She was great. We had a lot of fun and she was just perfect.'

Despite her bungled routines, Nancy survived the bottom two every week until she finally fell foul of the public vote in week five. But as he proved with Ann Widdecombe and Kate Garraway, Anton always manages to entertain, whatever his partner's ability. 'That's what it's all about really,' he says. 'It's hoping the public enjoy the show. If I want to dance with a fabulous dancer, I'll dance with Erin.'

Anton grew up in Sevenoaks, Kent, with a Spanish mother and a Hungarian father. At 14, he went to pick up his sister from a ballroom class and, seeing a room full of girls, decided to swap his football boots for dancing shoes. He trained in Latin and ballroom until he was 17 when he chose to specialise in ballroom.

In order to pay for his dancing. Anton worked as a baker, getting up at 3 a.m. and training in the evenings, before moving into retail and later interior design. He is one of three professionals – along with his partner Erin Boag and Brendan Cole – who have been with the show since its start, in 2004, and he still loves every minute of it.

'It's just the joy of doing it and the process,' he says. 'I enjoy it enormously, spending time with the celebrity, doing the show on Saturday night and then hoping to get them through to come back for another week. It's fun trying to come up with something inventive and new and interesting, and if we can do some good dancing along the way that's all the better.'

For the tenth series, Anton is looking forward to 'fun, enjoyment. I always get on with my celebrities and I want them to have a great time. The main thing for me is that they enjoy the experience of *Strictly Come Dancing*.'

But he admits he would like to get to the final – a treat that has eluded him so far. 'I desperately want to do a showdance!' he says. 'Then I'll know I've made the final.'

Strictly QUIZ

1

In week one Len told Robbie Savage, 'There have been three footballers so far on *Strictly* – and you're the best.' In fact Robbie was the fourth. Can you name the others?

2

What stunt did Ann Widdecombe perform in her series eight tango with Anton?

3

Which series three contestant did Craig call a 'sluggish dead weight and a noose around Brendan's neck'?

4

Which three professionals have partnered a celebrity in all nine series?

5

Aliona lifted the glitterball with Harry in series nine. Where did she come in the previous series?

6

Which dance had John Sergeant performed when Craig told him 'You took marching to a whole new level'?

7

Who were the first King and Queen of *Strictly Come Dancing*?

8

Which couple's charleston to 'Fat Sam's Grand Slam' was a smash hit in series seven?

9

Which series six contestant missed a week's dancing after catching chicken pox?

10

Which former contestant stood in for Tess when she was on maternity leave in 2005?

11

Name the original judging panel of *Strictly*.

12

Which two former EastEnders were first to end their *Strictly* dream in series six?

13

Two chefs have brought tasty treats to the dance floor. Can you name them?

14

Which cricketer bowled the judges over with a foxtrot and a paso doble to take the series three trophy?

15

Which celebrity did Craig compare to 'a bush kangaroo' in series seven?

16

Who leads the 'wonderful orchestra' introduced by Bruce each week?

17

What unusual mode of transport did Matt Baker use in his charleston in series eight?

18

Whose initial dance to 'Could It Be Magic' failed to cast a spell on Bruno, who commented, 'You got the wrong song. It should have been Could It Be Tragic!'?

19

Which comedian stood in for Bruce Forsyth for the only show he has missed, in 2009?

20

Two years before winning series eight, Kara Tointon had danced in a Sports Relief special. Which former winner was her partner?

Prima Donna

New judge Darcey Bussell brings a wealth of dance experience to the judging panel, as well as adding a dash of glamour. But the prima ballerina promises she'll be no pushover when it comes to the critique on a Saturday night...

Will you be a harsh judge?

I am quite critical if somebody has potential and I see that they are not doing a good enough job, then I will tell them where they're going wrong. But I don't want to put them down to the extent that they don't want to dance again. People get competitive at the end but at the beginning the nerves take over so much and I'm very sympathetic on that score. Being a performer all my life, I understand what it's like to step into a zone which is not your own.

Have you been swotting up on ballroom and Latin rules?

I can't help but swot up and I enjoy learning different styles but my comments will be much more on the performance side. Len is the technician and he knows every detail of that. For me, it will be about the musicality and style.

Last time you were on the show you did a jive with Ian Waite. How did it feel to be in the contestant's shoes?

It was terrifying! I would never have done it if I knew I was going to be judged. It was really exciting and Ian was a gorgeous partner but it was a great challenge, especially dancing in the heels, which I found really unnerving on the dance floor. I'm a bit spoilt this time because I get to do another dance with Ian – this time the American smooth. It's more in keeping with my dancing because it has a lyrical side to it. But the training was agony! My body really felt it.

How do you feel about becoming a judge on the show?

I can't wait. As guest judge I came in at the end so it was a lovely experience but I didn't feel that I saw the celebrities develop. I'm really looking forward to being there from the beginning and being part of the *Strictly* family. I've always been a big fan of the show and the positive light it sends out to the audience. It's uplifting.

How are you getting on with the other judges?

I got to dance with all the guys when we filmed the trailer. It was a lovely way of getting to know them better. They have all got such strong personalities and they're very different. I've known Craig for a while through his choreography. I get a little bit of jelly in the knees when I'm close to Len. I don't know Bruno well but he has enough energy for everyone so he's fun to be with. I just need to tell him to keep his hands to himself!

Darcey had a taste of *Strictly* in 2009, as a guest judge.

Nicky BYRNE

As a member of boyband Westlife, Nicky Byrne has thrown a few shapes on stage in front of huge arena crowds. But he is adamant that ballroom dancing is a new skill altogether.

'This is a lot more technical,' he explains. 'When we do the dance in the medleys, it's a bit tongue in cheek, with a lot of gyrating and pelvic thrusts, and it's just fun. We learn the routines together but if you look at the four of us, we do it all completely differently. If we were being judged for Westlife, we wouldn't be getting any sevens and eights!'

Dublin-born Nicky was a professional footballer, and played for Leeds United, before an audition with Boyzone manager Louis Walsh won him a place in Westlife in 1998, alongside Kian Egan, Mark Feehily, Shane Filan and Brian McFadden. Over the next 14 years the group sold over 45 million records worldwide, accumulated 14 number one singles and 26 top ten singles.

Having performed for the last time in June 2012, the remaining four members have gone their separate ways, but the lads are still behind Nicky's bid for *Strictly* glory. 'Shane is the one I've spoken to most recently and he says he's delighted for me,' he reveals. 'He was pushing me into doing it and said, "I'll come down and get you some votes." Kian texted me today and it would be great to get them down but it's very soon after we split. McFly came to the show every week for Harry but they're still a band, so it really depends what everybody is doing.'

Nicky, who is married to childhood sweetheart Georgina Ahern and has five-year-old twin sons, says he can take the comments of the judges on the chin, 'We were signed to Simon Cowell for 14 years so I know exactly what it's like to get criticism!'

But the 34-year-old singer is planning to put plenty of work in to the routines and is happy to be paired with new girl Karen Hauer. 'I'm looking forward to training actually,' he says. 'We only did two days for the launch show group dance and you learn a lot in two days but the individual training is when you really get stuck in to it.

'I've got a great partner. Karen was the first girl I danced with when we got in to group rehearsal and she was brilliant. She has a job on her hands but it should be fun.'

Karen HAUER

Venezuelan Vixen Karen Hauer is the new girl on the block but she has already settled in to the *Strictly* family. 'It's a bit nerve-wracking,' she admits, 'but since I know some of the dancers, they are embracing me like I've always been here. I have worked with Artem on *Burn the Floor* so it's great that he's my professional partner on the show. I also worked with Robin and Pasha and know Kristina and Aliona from the competition circuit, so in a way it doesn't feel like I am the new girl.'

Karen was born in Valencia, Venezuela and moved to New York with her family at eight. At her new primary school she entered an audition for a programme called Arts Connection, and got chosen to study African dance. 'I didn't know anything about dancing,' she recalls. 'I remember just doing a cartwheel and falling into a split, and I was wearing jeans. I was a tomboy who loved sports so that was my introduction to dance, and I loved all the music and the people that it introduced me to. I was having issues at home so I went into a little world of my own with my dancing.'

At ten, Karen won a scholarship to the Martha Graham School of Contemporary Dance, before moving on to 'Fame School' at La Guardia High School of the Performing Arts for dance.

'Ballroom came into my life when I was 19,' she continues. 'I remember going into a cha-cha-cha class in New Jersey and it just felt so natural. I grew up in a Latin environment so my family had parties and DJs and my mum loved to dance. She always wanted to be a dancer but her family was very poor and didn't really have the funds to take her to dance school.'

After taking up Latin dance, she became the American Rhythm National Champion and World Mambo Champion. She has also worked as a dancer for Jennifer Lopez and danced on *So You Think You Can Dance.*

Becoming a professional on *Strictly*, however, is a dream come true – and mum couldn't be prouder. 'She's amazed,' smiles Karen. 'She said, "It's not a little dream. It's a huge dream."'

The stunning dancer is looking forward to taking on her first *Strictly* celeb. 'I'm preparing my toes to get stepped on!' she laughs. 'And hoping he won't drop me. But I've been dropped before – you just get up and start again.'

While Karen loves all the dances, the Latin numbers still fire her up the most. 'My favourites are the mambo and the salsa. Salsa has been with me since I was a little girl, dancing it socially with my family, so now that I can actually do it as a professional it is special. It gives me goose bumps just thinking about it.'

Kimberley WALSH

Last year Chelsee Healey stole the show as *Shrek*'s Princess Fiona – but this year Pasha has the real thing. Kimberley Walsh is fresh from playing the fairy-tale heroine in the sell-out West End show – and it gave her the courage to take on the ballroom challenge.

'I had considered it in the past and there was always too much going on and I was a little bit scared of it probably,' she admits. 'And then doing *Shrek*, being terrified to do that but then loving it made me think I'd probably really love the experience if I can be brave enough to go for it, so I am! It's totally up my street, something I'll really enjoy, I'm sure I'll thoroughly embrace it.'

Bradford-born Kimberley shot to fame in 2002 when she made it into the final line-up of the girl group in *Popstars, The Rivals*. The five formed Girls Aloud and went on to have 20 consecutive top ten singles, including four number ones, and sell over 4.2 million albums.

Now her bandmates, including best pal Cheryl Cole, are backing her bid for the glitterball. 'I asked them before I signed up to it, and Cheryl basically told me I had to do it,' reveals the 30-year-old. 'She gave me no choice! They're really excited about it, they're really happy that I'm doing it. For them it's going to be great because they can just chill out and watch. They are really supportive of the decision, so they'll no doubt be coming down to cheer me on.'

Kimberley's pop career means she is ready for the judges' criticism and says, 'I must be pretty thick-skinned after being in this job for so many years.' But Pasha is in for a fight if he wants to choose all the tracks for the couple's dances. 'The music choice is quite a big thing; I'm probably going to be a bit bossy about that. For me it makes a massive difference if I love the song I'm performing to, so hopefully we get a bit of choice in the matter.'

After many TV appearances and tours, the Girls Aloud star is used to skimpy costumes and sexy dances but says she won't be getting too racy on *Strictly*. 'On tour we'd be dancing with partners and I'm used to that stuff which is good,' she says. 'But I don't think you need to raunch it up – the costumes are bad enough! We'll be toning it down.'

Pasha KOVALEV

As last year's new boy, Pasha made an impressive *Strictly* debut – taking Chelsee Healey all the way to the finals and finishing as runner up. 'I had so much fun with Chelsee,' recalls the Russian. 'I am so happy that I got her because she was a little firecracker.'

The *Waterloo Road* actress blossomed throughout the series and landed a perfect score for her semi-final paso doble. 'She improved amazingly and that's the appeal of the show, to take raw material and make them presentable and look like dancers,' says Pasha. 'Chelsee had an inner talent and I just had to tweak it a little bit so I was lucky.'

Despite losing out to Harry and Aliona, Pasha enjoyed the close-run final. 'I wasn't disappointed,' he says. 'Harry and Aliona were great competitors and dancing against them in the final was brilliant. Chelsee did her part and I think it was a very strong final. Winning is good and I like the idea but more important for me is to deliver a beautiful performance and get Chelsee to believe deep down that she can come out there and do something that she's never done before.'

Pasha was born in Siberia and fell in love with dance when his mum took him to watch a ballroom competition at the age of eight. Growing up as a dancer in Russia earned him more respect than ridicule from his peers. 'It is as prestigious to be a dancer as to be a football player and maybe that's why Russia is very famous for raising great dancers known around the whole world,' he explains. After reaching the finals of *So You Think You Can Dance* in the USA, Pasha performed in the Broadway and West End productions of *Burn The Floor*, before joining *Strictly*.

Pasha admits his first year on the show was 'tiring' but wouldn't have it any other way. 'I was prepared for the fact that it would be intense and it was more intense than I thought, but it's also very rewarding,' he says. 'You come out and do what you love to do, you work hard, it keeps you in shape and you get to open up and be creative which I love to do.'

This season he's hoping to build on last year's success. 'If I could get Chelsee again that would be perfect,' he says. 'I just want someone who is not afraid to experiment and be open to dance ideas, who will work hard – and stay off the phone.'

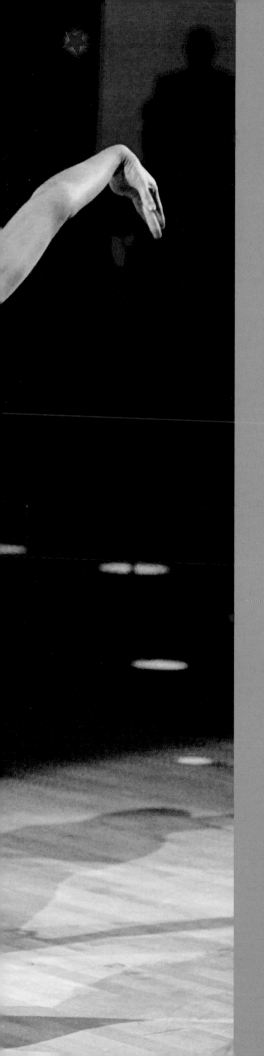

Dancing WITH THE STARS

The American version of the show, **Dancing With The Stars**, kicked off its fourteenth season with a glittering cast including Martina Navratilova, Melissa Gilbert and Gladys Knight. But it was a sprinkling of Welsh magic that set this season apart.

Katherine THE GREAT

She has sung on the shows on both sides of the Atlantic but earlier this year, **Katherine Jenkins** went from Welsh warbler to dance floor diva as she took *Dancing With The Stars* by storm.

Paired with two-time champion Mark Ballas in the US version of *Strictly*, Katherine admitted to being daunted by the dancing in the first few weeks. 'Even though I sing in front of millions of people, dancing in front of millions of people scares the living daylights out of me,' she said. 'When I sing it's me standing in one spot. This is completely different for me. I'm definitely out of my comfort zone.'

But the blonde bombshell won the judges over in week one, with a fabulous foxtrot which had Carrie Ann Inaba gasping, 'best first dance on first episode ever.' Fellow judge Bruno Tonioli added, 'where are we going to go from here? You are setting the bar so high, you have a lot to live up to.'

But the mezzo-soprano did just that, staying at the top of the leader board for the first three weeks and leaving her fellow competitors – who included singer Gladys Knight, tennis ace Martina Navratilova and *Little House on the Prairie* star Melissa Gilbert – to gaze in awe. Knocked off the top spot in week four, after a less-than-perfect paso doble, Katherine was back on fighting form the following week. The passionate Argentine tango had head judge Len waxing lyrical: 'This for me was like a rose. It has beauty but underneath the surface is the thorn – sharp, menacing, bittersweet.' Carrie Ann called it 'poetry in motion' and a score of 29 out of 30 was in the bag.

Paso Diva: Katherine and Mark grab the limelight with their Spanish steps.

The three *Dancing With the Stars* finalists and their partners.

In week eight, Katherine and Mark joined forces with eliminated professional Tristan MacManus for the first ever *Dancing With The Stars* threesome cha-cha-cha but the dance almost ended in disaster when the two men went to rip her suit off to reveal a Latin outfit – and Katherine was left to dance on with half the trousers hanging off her ankle.

With an unchoreographed kick, she rid herself of the offending trouser leg and impressed Len. 'You had that wardrobey thing but you kicked it off, carried on with the dance and it was clean, it was clear and it was clever,' he commented.

'It was sheer terror,' said Katherine later. 'It was wrapped around my ankle and I was worried I was going to fall.'

The following week, disaster struck again when the singer's back went into spasm during her semi-final samba and she couldn't carry on. Afterwards, the tearful contestant told her worried partner, 'I just felt my back go as I bent. I'm so sorry if I've let you down.' But the judges were full of comfort, with Bruno gushing, 'you unleashed the harlot which is good to see. Don't worry about what happened because it could happen to anybody. Up to that point it was absolutely wonderful.'

With the wardrobe malfunction and injury behind her, the Welsh Wriggler, as partner Mark dubbed her, went powering on to the finals. And she gave the audience a show to remember – with three dances and three perfect scores.

The first dance was the judges' choice and the tough trio chose the paso doble, Katherine's most disappointing dance of the season. But after a lesson from Len she got some flamenco flame into her belly and went for the final hurdle. She said: 'I've never had a ten from Len so I'm hoping if I listen to everything he says and really take it on, I have more of a chance.'

Above: Katherine proved a hit with her final freestyle and week one foxtrot. Right: Donald Driver pipped Katherine to the post and claimed the trophy in the final.

Bruno said it was a 'paso doble full of vivid, lush, lustrous artistry' and all three reached for the maximum score paddle. Then came a sizzling show dance which Carrie called 'the dance of a champion'. Finally the couple had 24 hours to come up with a new jive, and they still knocked the socks off the judging panel with Len calling Katherine, 'the complete package' and Bruno dubbing her 'the blonde bombshell, the girl who has it all.'

With 90 out of 90, Katherine and Mark topped the table with Donald Driver and William Levy just one point behind. Willam and partner Cheryl Burke were first out. Then came the moment of truth. After an agonising wait, Katherine was dealt a bitter blow – as American footballer Donald Driver and Peta Murgatroyd scooped the glitterball trophy.

'It's been an absolute dream,' Katherine said, as she gracefully accepted defeat. But for head judge Len

Goodman, the public had made the wrong choice.

'Katherine was fantastic,' he said. 'She should have won. She was incredible. If you ask me the best dancer on *Strictly*, I would say Alesha Dixon, but if you ask me who's the best girl I've seen on both shows I would either go with Katherine Jenkins or Nicole Scherzinger. But American Football players are very popular there and they get the best. It's a bit like having David Beckham taking part because that's how big their profiles are.'

Despite losing out to the NFL star, Katherine was delighted by the reception she received from the US audience. 'It's just crazy because when I came here nobody knew me and now I go out for dinner and people are talking about dancing,' she said. 'I feel very welcomed here and it's so nice to come to a new country and feel like people have embraced you. It's just been an amazing time and I've loved every minute of it.'

Richard ARNOLD

Following in the faltering footsteps of Fiona Phillips, Kate Garraway and Andrew Castle, Richard will be hoping to break the curse of former *GMTV* presenters. But the showbiz reporter hasn't turned to his ex-colleagues for advice – which is probably wise.

'I haven't told a soul about *Strictly*,' he says. 'I know how nervous they all were and I could see the fear in their eyes every Friday before they were due to take part, as palpable as their relief on the Monday when they'd survived another week. Not one of them regrets it, though, and I know they still miss the frocks. Andrew Castle especially, but then he has the physique of a tennis pro.'

The Hampshire-born journalist worked on TV magazines before becoming a regular critic on *GMTV* in 1997. After leaving 13 years later, he presented his own shows, including *Loose Lips* and *The Planet's Funniest Animals* before returning to morning telly as Showbiz Editor on *Daybreak*.

Richard is looking forward to some verbal sparring with the judges, especially a certain arch Australian. 'Craig and I are both renowned for our verbal gymnastics so it should be interesting,' he says. 'I've met Craig a couple of times through the job and we do enjoy a fine line in banter when we meet. Just wait until he sees my jazz kick!'

The flamboyant presenter was looking forward to the sparkle and spangles of the costumes, but he admits he got a bit of a shock at his first wardrobe call.

'Up until my costume fitting I was excited about the lustre and the Lycra. But then I discovered that the Latin pants cut you higher than is faintly decent, and saw a muffin top in the mirror Delia would be proud of,' he laughs. 'It dawned on me that it's not everyone who can carry off marabou under a mirror ball on a Saturday night. It didn't help that they put me in to Robbie Savage's old costume and he's an Adonis. Then they had to cut the shirt right up the back just to let out the muffin top!'

The 42-year-old admits to a passion for dairy products which he is hoping partner Erin will be helping him to work off in the training room. 'I can't have butter in the house because I will slice through it like cheese,' he confesses. 'If I so much as look at a lump of brie I will run to fat. I'm only in this show to drop a dress size before Christmas!'

Erin BOAG

Rory Bremner made a great impression on Erin in the last series, but it ended in tears when the couple were early victims of the public vote, going out in week four. 'Every year, there's one that goes too soon and one that stays longer than they should,' says Erin. 'Rory went too soon and he got emotional about it, because we had so much more.'

Erin was one of the original professionals, kicking off in the first series with rugby star Martin Offiah, then coming third with Julian Clary and coming within a hair's breadth of the trophy in the final of series three, with Colin 'Snake hips' Jackson.

'The people on the first series were the guinea pigs and it was an unknown quantity,' she recalls. 'And it worked. But if you'd said to me "You're still going to be there ten series later, and the show is bigger and better than ever," I wouldn't have believed it.'

Erin grew up in Auckland, New Zealand, where her parents were professional ballroom dancers. At three, she was learning ballet, tap, jazz, Latin and ballroom and carried on dancing through her teens, as well as representing her school in swimming, hockey, netball, football, trampolining and athletics.

A 10-Dance champion by 18, she moved to Sydney to compete for 18 months before travelling across the world to London. She told her mum she would be a couple of months – and hasn't left since. In 1997, she met Anton Du Beke and formed a dance partnership that would have them competing in the Royal Albert Hall within the year.

Erin is looking forward to her tenth series of *Strictly* and, although she would love to lift the trophy, this girl just wants to have fun.

'I have come to the conclusion that it's better getting someone loveable that you can have a good time with, over someone who really wants to win,' she says. 'I have been fortunate over the nine seasons that I've had really nice men. Whether they could dance or not is beside the point! The professionals are with their celebrities every day and you have to want to go into the studio and to have fun when you're there because it makes your job easier. I have always had that and I hope to be in that position again. Tenth time lucky? I don't know.'

Lisa RILEY

Best known as *Emmerdale* legend Mandy Dingle, a role she played for over six years, Lisa Riley had trodden the boards on numerous occasions but reckons her theatre experience won't help her in the ballroom.

'The others should not be worried - AT ALL!' she laughs. 'The first couple of weeks I will definitely be totally two-left-footed, but I think we all will. I've done a bit of dancing before in a couple of shows, but this is totally different. It's like a comedy-drama actor suddenly having to learn Shakespeare.'

Lisa was born in Bury, Lancashire and took up acting at the age of nine, at Oldham Theatre Workshop. After extra roles in *Coronation Street*, she joined the cast of *Emmerdale* in 1995 and went on to present *You've Been Framed* as well as starring in ITV drama *Fat Friends*.

The 36-year-old actress lost her mum to breast cancer earlier this year but says she will be spurred on by her memory. 'I think my mum will be on my shoulder keeping an eye on me and with me every step of the way,' she says. 'It was one of her absolute favourite shows.'

As well as challenging herself, Lisa signed up to show everyone that size doesn't matter. 'I want to prove that big girls can be funky and have a ball dancing,' she explains. 'Anywhere you go in the country, people of any shape and size can dance and why not?'

Her pairing with British beefcake, Robin, has thrilled her for similar reasons. 'On day one we clicked, straight away, and I knew our personalities would work together and with those muscles – well, he's got to get me off the ground hasn't he! I'm made up. I secretly had my fingers crossed for him.'

As well as learning some new steps for *Strictly*, Lisa is preparing for a whole new look. 'I've never had a spray tan in my life!' she says. 'I'm frightened of looking like an Oompa Loompa! I don't want to look shiny – I am incredibly pale so I think I might look a bit ridiculous but I'm going to throw myself into the *Strictly* experience 100%.'

Even so, she has some words of warning for the judges. 'If they criticise me, they'll have to remember I was a Dingle. You know what happens – straight in the face!'

Robin WINDSOR

The only problem Robin had with series nine partner Anita Dobson was wiping the smile off her face. The joy the former *EastEnders* actress found when on the dance floor was written all over it.

'Whoever I get this year has got a lot to live up to, to be as wonderful and lovely as Anita,' says Robin. 'She had this huge love of what we do as a profession and you could see that week after week after week. She just loved it every single week and she never wanted it to end. I have a friend for life.'

At 62, she was one of the older competitors but she wasn't letting age slow her down.

'Every single moment I've spent with her – whether we're dancing or not – she is just full of life, full of vitality,' he marvels. 'She tired *me* out. She's an inspiration for so many people.'

Robin was born near Ipswich and started dancing at the age of three. He attended The Ipswich School of Dance where he initially trained in ballroom before specialising in Latin. At 15, he moved to London to continue his training and compete in youth competitions. Before joining the *Strictly* professionals, Robin toured for nine years with *Burn The Floor*, performing all around the world including the West End and Broadway.

The beefy Brit was paired with Patsy Kensit in his first year on *Strictly*, and thinks that actresses make good dance partners. 'I've been very lucky to have two actresses in two years because where they might struggle on technique, they can sell it elsewhere with acting,' he explains. 'I'd love a sports star. I think that would be really challenging because they're people who have never been to stage school, or dance classes, so you're starting from scratch. They're also fit and determined. From what I hear, sports stars will just keep going and going until they get it 100 per cent right, or as right as they can get it.'

'I'd love to have somebody who's capable of some crazy stuff because I've got a lot inside I want to let out but you have to have the right partner to be able to do some of these things.'

After two years falling just short of the quarter-finals, Rocking Robin is ready to go all the way this year. 'Both years it's been week nine, so I'm hoping to at least go further than that and the Final's in my sights,' he says. 'There's a big space on my mantelpiece for that glitterball!'

WHAT GOES ON

As most of the contestants soak their aching feet in iced water and take a well-earned rest at the end of the series, a few hardy souls resolve to 'keeeeeep dancing' on the annual tour. Craig Revel Horwood, who directs the spectacular show, has to have the soothsaying skills of Russell Grant to decide who to book.

'I pick the celebrities in October, never knowing what the outcome of *Strictly* is going to be,' he explains. 'So far it's worked out really well every time. I had no idea that Harry Judd was going to win, or that Chelsee would come second and Jason third. I just knew I wanted those personalities on the tour.'

The other series nine celebs with a seat on the 2012 tour bus were Anita Dobson, Robbie Savage and the inimitable Nancy Dell'Olio. The lucky lady got to dance with both Artem and Robin – and was literally treated like a queen.

'I invited Nancy Dell'Olio on tour because of her immaculate dancing skills!' laughs Craig. 'We made her Cleopatra and brought her out on a sedan, carried by two muscle boys which thankfully used up two minutes of dance time. Then she went into an Egyptian salsa which actually doesn't exist but we created it for the tour.

'Her banter was brilliant and the audience loved it because she was acting like she deserved to be anointed and bathed in the tears of a Tibetan yak. She was fun to have on tour because she was basically playing herself!'

Nancy Dell'Olio makes a characteristic entrance for her 'Egyptian salsa'.

TOUR

Natalie was delighted to be dancing with Olympian Mark Foster.
Opposite page: Robbie Savage got mixed reactions from the different audiences.

Artem took over as Nancy's main partner, in both the salsa and the tango, and he says he had a good time with the Italian diva. 'I didn't know what to expect,' he says. 'We had a couple of rehearsals before the tour and I was very surprised because she was dedicated, extremely nice and wanted to rehearse 24/7. It was never quite the same choreography but people seemed to like it.'

The final celebrity to join the line-up was series six contestant Mark Foster, who was paired with Natalie Lowe for the tour. 'There some amazing personalities who have been in the show and it's always good to mix the old with the new,' says Craig. 'Mark was great because the Olympics was coming up, he's a world champion swimmer and you can't get better than that. Plus we needed someone tall for Natalie Lowe to dance with and he's got the body to die for – who wouldn't want to see that shirt ripped off?'

Natalie wasn't complaining either.

'Mark was one of my most favourite partners ever!' she reveals. 'He is the most genuine, down to earth person you'll ever meet. He tried every night to be better and better and we were getting 9s and 10s at the end. I get goosebumps just thinking about it.

'I've made a really true friend for the rest of my life and I also danced with my best friend Ian Waite – what more could a girl want?'

The live tour kicked off in February and played more than forty dates around the country, including Scotland and Wales – where Robbie made very different impacts.

'Harry won most nights and Chelsee did really well,' recalls Craig. 'Robbie won in Wales but the best part was Robbie being booed in Scotland. It was the loudest boo I've heard since I slated Kenny Logan's kilted paso doble. The reverberations then shook the venue. But when Robbie started slagging off Scottish football everyone was chanting "Off! Off!" It was hideous but brilliant.

'The audience participation is part of the fun. You don't really get that unless you go to panto but this is adult audience participation, where they can boo if they want, cheer if they want, scream and yell "Fab-u-lous" and "se-VEN". It's become part of the British psyche and it's great to see it first-hand.'

The arena venues mean that fans who can't get tickets for the TV show get their own taste of the *Strictly* experience with all the excitement of the series, both off stage and on.

'This was one of the best tours we've ever had backstage and we all just gelled and got on,' says Craig. 'Although it's the same dances every night, it is a different show because someone could slip over or make a mistake and the comments are different. As on *Strictly Come Dancing*, it may go well on Friday but when it comes to performing on Saturday you could fall down the stairs or go blank. It's interesting for the audience because you get the whole feeling of the show and although they are huge venues with big screens you feel bizarrely intimate.

'It's very spectacular, requires an enormous amount of rehearsal but everybody had a laugh from beginning to end.'

The set, which has to be dismantled and shipped to each new venue, was bigger and better than before and the whole show was more explosive.

'We had lots of pyrotechnics,' says the director. 'Some fun video stuff and more props, like Nancy's coffin. We had great music and this year I put all the singers centre stage, because they are insanely talented so I wanted to highlight them. I wanted the audience to come out of the show feeling like they'd seen a massive event, like a rock concert but with incredible dances.'

It wasn't only the competing couples that got to dance on the 2012 tour. Craig choreographed a paso doble where Len danced with hostess Kate Thornton and Craig danced with Bruno!

'Bruno played the girl even though he said I did,' laughs Craig. 'I'm taller so I was the boy. Bruno was freaking out but he loved it in the end.'

Strictly ON SONG

Tony Bennett is among the many singing legends Tommy has met on the show.

Rarely seen but always heard, the *Strictly* singers are an integral part of the show. Along with the melodic input of Dave Arch and his orchestra, their soaring vocals provide a live musical backdrop to each couple's performance and set the mood for every dance. Between them, the talented foursome covers every type of song, from rock ballad and modern pop to big band classics and Latin mambo.

Lead singer Tommy Blaze joined the *Strictly* family on day one after being asked to audition by former Musical Director Laurie Holloway. Over 1500 songs later, he still gets a thrill out of performing live – and still gets the jitters every time.

'I love going in on a Saturday,' he says. 'Everyone is so focused on making the greatest show possible. We all get a little nervous just before we go on. There's a silent ten minutes because we know what we're about to do. I get the shakes but that's good. If I don't get nervous it's not as good a show.'

Band leader and former session singer Tommy specialises in soul music and ballads, and he's joined by jazz genius Hayley Sanderson, soul diva Andrea Grant and regular contributor Lance Ellington – a master of big band and jazz. Occasionally other artists are brought in to cover hard rock vocals or classical but Tommy admits that one band's songs gets them rattled.

'Whenever a Queen song comes up we always get nervous,' he reveals. 'And it was even worse last year because Anita Dobson was on the show so we had Brian May in every week, and more Queen songs to sing. On one show I shook his hand and said, "I'm really sorry, Brian." He replied, "You're doing a great job," which was lovely.'

By the time the show goes on air the quartet are always pitch perfect but, amazingly, they don't get together to rehearse until the day of the show.

'We get in for 7.30 or 8 a.m. so we can check the harmonies before the band gets in, because we don't want to waste any time getting it right on the bandstand. By the time we go live we've sung each song about four or five times, so the voice has already been through it. I can never hold back in rehearsal, we

DAVE ARCH ON THE SINGERS

'Tommy is brilliant. He has a great range, they all do. And they inherently understand all the different styles that are thrown at them. A lot of singers are just a soul singer, or a jazz singer, but they have to do all of that and their ability to grab the track and do it in the correct style is amazing.'

tend to just go for it and hope we've got a little bit of reserve left.

'There have been a few croaks and I've learned not to beat myself up, because it's live and we're doing 15 songs a week. Luckily I haven't had any big mess ups where I walk away saying, "ten million people just heard me hit that bum note!"'

Being focused on the task in hand, Tommy rarely watches the dancing but, from the orchestra pit at the side of the stage, he gets to see the weekly guest stars and has met a few of his idols.

'Tony Bennett was one, and it was amazing to meet him. I was in awe. I love all those old-fashioned singers. Andy Williams was another one. He came on in his little tight suit and trainers, in his mid-seventies, singing live and knocking out songs like he was 20 years old. Shirley Bassey was fabulous too.

'Even Bruce said I've got the best seat in the house and I have. I feel like the luckiest bloke in the world sitting in that chair.'

Tommy (centre left) is joined by Hayley Sanderson (left) and Lance Ellington (right)

Sid OWEN

Sid is a familiar face to soap fans, having played *EastEnders* Jack-the-lad Ricky for 25 years. He's also a culinary expert, having run his own restaurant in France and published a cookery book called *Life on a Plate: The Journey of an Unlikely Chef*. But can he cook up a storm on the dance floor? He's not convinced.

'I don't think I'm a very good dancer,' he confesses. 'Even at parties I'm the boring one who stands at the bar and hardly moves, I just sway in time to the music at the side and stay off the dance floor!'

Londoner Sid went to Anna Scher Stage School as a boy, and landed the role of Ricky when he was 16. He left the show to pursue a pop career in 2000 before returning to TV in 2002 and appearing in *I'm A Celebrity Get Me Out Of Here* in 2005, coming third in the series. He starred as a prison officer in the final series of *Bad Girls* before returning to Albert Square again in 2008.

The 40-year-old actor, who has now left the show again, is the latest in a long line of *EastEnders* to take the *Strictly* challenge. 'I've seen my co-stars take part for the last ten years,' says Sid. 'Jill Halfpenny won the second series and they have all really enjoyed it, so I thought it was my time to give it a go! Scott Maslen gave me a little bit of advice but it was all too much information to take on board. Everyone else just said "enjoy it" and that's all you can do.'

Sid reckons Ola has her work cut out turning him into a twinkle-toed hoofer but he is prepared to put the hours in to please her. 'From Ola, I suppose I am looking for patience most of all,' he admits. 'I'm not a dancer so I feel like a bit of an underdog, but it gives me more motivation to work hard and get better.'

As mechanic Ricky, Sid has spent most of his time on television in greasy overalls with an oil-splattered face, so he's keen to get the glamour on for his dance routines.

'I am really looking forward to the whole experience,' he says. 'But mainly learning to dance and getting dressed up in all the outfits every weekend. I can't wait to get into some sequins for this programme because it's all part of the fun. And maybe some leggings!'

Victoria PENDLETON

Having scooped silver and gold at the London Olympics, cyclist Victoria is looking to add some more bling to her trophy cabinet, in the shape of the coveted glitterball.

'I'm really looking forward to *Strictly*,' she admits. 'It will be me trying something new and also getting to dress very glamorously with all the sparkles and make-up and hair. I'm used to wearing a skin-suit, tying my hair back and looking all sweaty and dishevelled so it will be nice to be glamorised.'

Victoria was born in Bedfordshire, the daughter of a former grass-track cycling champion. She rode her first race when she was nine and, despite being picked for the National Track Team as a teenager, she concentrated on her studies until she graduated, with a Sports Degree, from Northampton University. She won her first Olympic gold at Beijing in 2008, for the Women's Individual Sprint event. The reigning world champion, she went on to earn two more Olympic medals in 2012, before retiring from racing.

For 'Queen Victoria', *Strictly* is the perfect antidote to the post-Olympic blues but she admits her dancing skills are a bit more wobbly than her cycling.

'I'm going to give myself 0.5 out of 10 for dancing but only for the fact that I'm not frightened to have a laugh at myself. I'll go out there and give it a go. If I was at a party and among friends then I'd definitely have a bit of a boogie but other than that not so much.'

But she has a very special reason to learn – her wedding to former coach Scott Gardner. 'Expectations will be very high now for our first dance!' she says. 'My fiance Scott is already feeling the pressure, but I reckon Scott's quite good; he has more dance skills already than I have.'

The athletic background makes her the perfect partner for slave-driver Brendan. 'Training for anything takes time and dedication,' she says. 'I know I'm going to want to practise *a lot*.'

The 32-year-old sportswoman may have ditched the bike for the ballroom but she is still eyeing up the competition – especially fellow Team GB Member, gymnast Louis Smith.

'I am annoyed they put another athlete in - especially one that can probably dance loads better than I can!' she jokes. 'And he can also do tricks! He's going to be flipping on to the dance floor. So I'm slightly intimidated by Louis. I have no dance experience, which is slightly concerning. I just hope people might feel sorry for me.'

Brendan COLE

New Zealander Brendan waltzed off with the first ever *Strictly* trophy, with newsreader Natasha Kaplinsky, and has had mixed fortunes ever since. Knocked out in week five the following year with Sarah Manners, he admitted, 'We deserved to get knocked out. It's not often I say that, I'm very competitive. We didn't really gel on or off the floor.'

A stint with the less-than-graceful Fiona Phillips saw him knocked out fourth and *Emmerdale* actress Claire King got him to week eight, but things looked like they were picking up when he was paired with the beautiful Kelly Brook – who proved pretty nimble on her feet, too. Sadly, due to the death of her father, the couple dropped out in week eight and Brendan is convinced they would have made the final.

Another great chance came with Lisa Snowdon, who got him to the final in series six, but ended in third place.

Partnerships with Jo Wood and Michelle Williams have seen the controversial hoofer fall short of the final and he reached week six with Lulu in series nine.

Brendan grew up in Christchurch, New Zealand, where he and his brother Scott enrolled in dance classes when he was six. Even though he hated dancing, and would be dragged there by his mum, he went on to become the Juvenile, Junior and Youth Champion of New Zealand. His younger sister Zoe had joined in the family dance craze and at one point his brother and sister were New Zealand No.1s, and Brendan was No.5.

At 18, the ambitious teen moved to the UK where he met Camilla Dallerup, who became his partner, on and off the dance floor, for eight years. After turning professional they taught in Hong Kong before both signing up for the first series of *Strictly*.

Brendan, who is married to model Zoe Hobbs, is hoping to make his lone trophy part of a matching pair and asks only one thing of his partner. 'I hope she's as competitive as I am,' he says.

Divas & Disasters

Although every *Strictly* celebrity puts in time, hard work and a whole lot of commitment, there is no substitute for the two most crucial ingredients – raw talent and a sense of rhythm. Over nine series, the studio has seen everything from dancefloor delights to downright disasters. For every Kara Tointon or Harry Judd, there's an Ann Widdecombe or Nancy Dell'Olio waiting in the wings. But the viewers love a tryer – as long as they keep it entertaining. So let's celebrate the fabulous footwork and ballroom blunders that have kept millions coming back for more.

RAMPRAKASH MAKES HIS MARK Cricketer Mark Ramprakash turned catastrophe into conquest with his series five salsa. When they first performed it in week five, Mark's microphone got caught in partner Karen Hardy's dress and they were forced to stop. For the first and only time, a couple were allowed to start the routine again. It earned them 36 and went on to gain them a perfect score in the Grand Final, bagging the trophy.

DOBLE DISGRACE Series two celeb Chris Parker bagged the lowest score ever for his clod-hopping paso doble, which included a lap of honour round the dance floor, waving a cape. He hung on to the record, with 22 points, but lost out in the most memorable paso stakes when John Sergeant dragged Kristina round the floor in his series six matador tribute. Len told him, 'Sergeant, after all that marching you should be demoted to a private!'

WIDDECOMBE DANCING Former MP Ann Widdecombe holds the record for the lowest score for the most dances. She came bottom in the opinion polls, as far as the judges were concerned, for the American smooth, charleston, samba and salsa, for which she scored her personal worst of 12 points. Bruno described the dance as, 'unique and compelling, somewhere between horror and comedy.'

SNOW QUEEN Despite coming third in series six, Lisa Snowdon and Brendan Cole hold the record for the most perfect scores, managing four 40s. They are also the only couple to have achieved four 10s for a cha-cha-cha, which Bruno called 'truly eye-poppingly brilliant.'

LEARNER DRIVER Motor-mad Quentin Wilson, presenter of *Britain's Worst Drivers,* failed to get into gear when it came to his series two cha-cha-cha, and still holds the record for the lowest scored dance of all nine series. His Latin lumberings bagged him just eight points and Craig dubbed him 'Britain's Worst Dancer.'

JIVING JILL Series two winner Jill Halfpenny was the first celebrity to earn a perfect score, for her Grand Final jive to Elton John's 'I'm Still Standing'. And for that dance, at least, the record still stands.

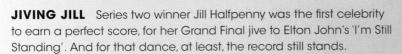

CHELSEE'S SPANISH SENSATION Series nine runners up Chelsee Healey and Pasha Kovalev are the only couple to score full marks for their paso doble in the semi-finals. Bruno said it was, 'like the build-up of a storm in the plains of Andalucia. Fantastic.'

JASON'S JIVE JITTERS Jason Donovan's jive to 'Wake Me Up Before You Go-go', at Wembley Arena, was exquisitely timed until he forgot a whole kicks and flicks section near the end. Bruno told him, 'up until you lost it, it was amazing.' The talented Aussie later admitted, 'the situation did overwhelm me but I really enjoyed it.'

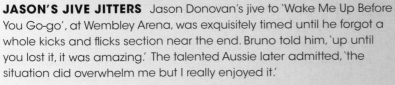

DIARMUID AND DISASTER Garden designer Diarmuid Gavin wasn't coming up roses on the dance floor in series two. He stayed for four dances, three of which were the lowest scoring of the series and two – the tango and the quickstep – remain the lowest scoring ever for those dances. Craig told him , 'you possess absolutely no dance talent whatsoever.'

FUMBLING FIONA *GMTV* star Fiona Phillips scored three of the show's lowest scores when she lumbered her way through series three with 13 for her rumba, 16 for her jive and just 11 for her waltz, which Arlene told her 'was so awful I don't know what to say.'

EVEN STEVENS With 39, Rachel Stevens and partner Vincent Simone share the record for the rumba with Chelsee and Pasha and Kara Tointon and Artem Chigvintsev. This means the perfect rumba – one that pleases Craig enough for a 10 – is still up for grabs. Rachel is also the only celeb with a 39 for the tango and shares a record of the perfect score for the foxtrot with Lisa Snowdon.

SHOWING OFF Series seven runner up Ricky Whittle and series nine contestant Jason Donovan are the only two celebs to get full marks for their showdances – but neither of them bagged the trophy.

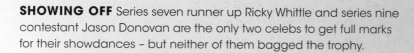

PERFECT PARTNERS Soap hunk Matt Di Angelo and partner Flavia Cacace had the judges in a lather over their semi-final waltz and still have the only perfect score for the dance. Series seven stars Ali Bastian and Brian Fortuna hold the same record for the American smooth and Chris Hollins and Ola Jordan have the only perfect charleston score.

STRICTLY *Style*

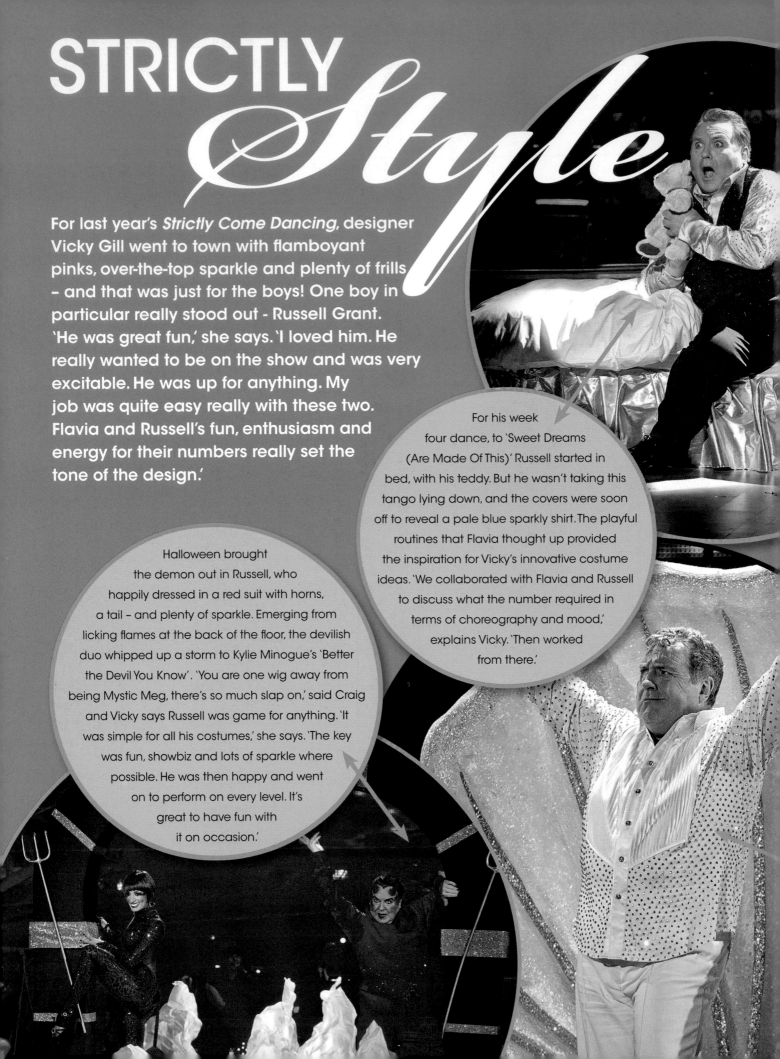

For last year's *Strictly Come Dancing*, designer Vicky Gill went to town with flamboyant pinks, over-the-top sparkle and plenty of frills – and that was just for the boys! One boy in particular really stood out - Russell Grant. 'He was great fun,' she says. 'I loved him. He really wanted to be on the show and was very excitable. He was up for anything. My job was quite easy really with these two. Flavia and Russell's fun, enthusiasm and energy for their numbers really set the tone of the design.'

For his week four dance, to 'Sweet Dreams (Are Made Of This)' Russell started in bed, with his teddy. But he wasn't taking this tango lying down, and the covers were soon off to reveal a pale blue sparkly shirt. The playful routines that Flavia thought up provided the inspiration for Vicky's innovative costume ideas. 'We collaborated with Flavia and Russell to discuss what the number required in terms of choreography and mood,' explains Vicky. 'Then worked from there.'

Halloween brought the demon out in Russell, who happily dressed in a red suit with horns, a tail – and plenty of sparkle. Emerging from licking flames at the back of the floor, the devilish duo whipped up a storm to Kylie Minogue's 'Better the Devil You Know'. 'You are one wig away from being Mystic Meg, there's so much slap on,' said Craig and Vicky says Russell was game for anything. 'It was simple for all his costumes,' she says. 'The key was fun, showbiz and lots of sparkle where possible. He was then happy and went on to perform on every level. It's great to have fun with it on occasion.'

Russell began his week seven American smooth in a sober grey suit – albeit with a little added sparkle. But after disappearing behind a screen he emerged in a show-stopping gold suit for a high-kicking finale to camp anthem 'I Am What I Am'. 'You were like a giant Ferrero Rocher dancing round the floor, and it made me laugh,' said Len. 'The gold suit was my favourite,' says Vicky. 'The suit was covered with sequins so that when he appeared from behind the screen his outfit was noticeably different - very showbiz and jazz hands.'

Russell kicked off his *Strictly* run by emerging from a shell dressed in a white shirt which sparkled with thousands of crystals, to the strains of Bananarama's 'Venus'. 'It's like watching Frankie Howerd do Bananarama,' said Bruno. 'You couldn't be camper if you tried.' But Russell loved nothing better than getting glitzed-up. 'We would not have had the budget for two characters like Russell in the crystal department,' laughs Vicky. 'We had to padlock the cupboard.'

Among the many amazing outfits in the last series, Vicky's favourite was the Black Swan look she created for Holly and Artem's memorable American smooth, on Halloween night. 'We loved the Black Swan theme,' says Vicky. 'It had light and shade and lots of drama!' The judges agreed, admiring both the dance and the costume. 'You both look incredible,' commented Alesha. 'This is my favourite concept so far.'

Nancy and Russell proved to be birds of a feather when both chose a boa for a routine, with comical consequences. The Italian diva got tangled in her fluffy accessory in her week one waltz, causing Anton to rename it a 'boa constrictor'. The following week the stargazer chose a pink boa to go with his outrageous blue silk shirt with pink and blue frills on the arms. But when he tried to unravel another boa from Flavia's skirt, he got in a tangle. Even so, Vicky says boas are not banned from the dance floor this year. 'It's not actually a wardrobe malfunction as it is not part of the costume, they were props,' she says. 'Wardrobe is an easy target when things go wrong but it's all part of the fun.'

The wardrobe department came up with some brand-new looks for the series – including Chelsee's flight attendant look, Anita's stunning black flapper dress and the elegant pink and gold ballgown Alex wore for her week three foxtrot. But Vicky insists all the celebrities were a joy to work with. 'No one was hard to dress,' she reveals. 'It's part of the challenge on *Strictly* to work with everyone's characters, shapes and abilities to arrive at the very best outcome for them. We do our best and on the whole they appreciate it.'

Harry came across as a shy lad at the beginning of the run but by week three he was getting his chest out for the *Grease* jive and biceps made an appearance on several occasions, including his week six samba. 'Coming from a boy band he could have been very precious about his look and costume options but he wasn't,' explains Vicky. 'Both Harry and Aliona collaborated with us to achieve a look that suited production's themes but still looked current, keeping a sense of style at all times.'

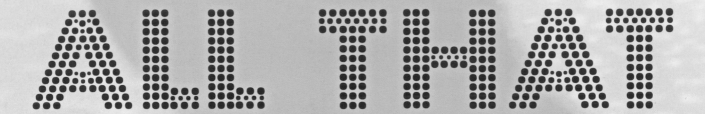

ALL THAT

It's the iconic trophy which every celebrity and dancer wants to get their hands on and its thousands of mirrors have reflected years of joy and tears. But there is only one man in possession of the real *Strictly Come Dancing* glitterball – props designer **BOBBY WARANS**

Bobby came up with the sparkling prize for series one, using a 10-inch ABS plastic and glass mirror ball designed to hang from a ceiling. Every year, two 6-inch replicas are made – one for each winner – with the latest gracing the mantelpieces of Harry and Aliona. In fact, they are so rare that not even Tess and Bruce possess a copy.

Here's how the *Strictly* trophy was made:

First, the hollow ABS mirror ball is removed from its ceiling fixture and bolted to a 16-inch clear acrylic rod which is fixed to a 6-inch square black acrylic base, so that the ball is suspended three inches above the top face of the cube.

The *Strictly Come Dancing* logo is cut out of a brass sheet. The letters are then finished by hand, using sandpaper, then softened with a blowtorch, before being bent by hand to fit the curve of the custom-made clear acrylic shroud which goes around the ball.

They are then primed with a red oxide acrylic spray, before being coated on both sides with the show's trademark purple – using paint designed for car bodywork.

Each letter is then glued onto the plastic shroud.

The shroud is bolted at three points around the equator of the mirror ball and the bolts sleeved with polished aluminium tube.

The trophy is then cleaned again and a brass plate is added, ready to bear the names of the lucky winners.

Glitterball Facts

The largest glitterball in the world is outside *Strictly's* second home, The Tower Ballroom in Blackpool. Constructed in 2000, it's 7.3 metres in diameter, weighs 4.5 tonnes and has 46,000 mirrored tiles. It goes by the curious name of They Shoot Horses Don't They?

Pink Floyd used massive glitterballs on two of their concert tours, in 1987 and 1994.

Madonna's 2006 Confessions tour featured a two-ton glitterball encrusted with £1.3 million worth of Swarovski crystals.

The largest disco ball ever made measures 9.98 metres in diameter, and was made by BSG Luxury Group for Bacardi, Russia. The ball was the centrepiece at the firm's Larger Than Life party in Moscow, on 26 April 2012.

The writing on the *Strictly* trophy was changed from pink to purple, to coincide with the redesign of the set in series eight.

GLITTERS

Above: the *Strictly* trophy before the series-eight redesign Left: even before the disco age, glitterballs graced the ceilings of many ballrooms.

History of the Glitterball

The name of the inventor is long forgotten, but the first mirror balls were thought to have decorated ballrooms in the US at the turn of the twentieth century. The earliest recorded mention appears in an 1897 article about a ball at Roughaus Hall in Boston, which describes a twinkling display caused by a light trained on a mirrored ball on the ceiling.

The popularity of the glitterball spread in the jazz era, with many nightclubs adopting them to delight their charleston-loving clientele in the Roaring Twenties. The first screen glimpse is in a nightclub scene of the German silent movie, *Berlin: Die Sinfonie der Großstadt* (*Berlin: Symphony of a Great City*), in 1927.

The disco age, in the 1970s and '80s, saw the sparkling spheres suspended from the ceilings of discos and nightclubs everywhere, but the birth of *Strictly Come Dancing* has bounced the ball firmly back into the ballroom.

YOU BE THE

		Colin & Kristina	Dani & Vincent	Johnny & Aliona	Denise & James	Louis & Flavia	Fern & Artem	Michael & Natalie
Show 1	Your Score							
	Judges' Score							
Show 2	Your Score							
	Judges' Score							
Show 3	Your Score							
	Judges' Score							
Show 4	Your Score							
	Judges' Score							
Show 5	Your Score							
	Judges' Score							
Show 6	Your Score							
	Judges' Score							
Show 7	Your Score							
	Judges' Score							
Show 8	Your Score							
	Judges' Score							
Show 9	Your Score							
	Judges' Score							
Show 10	Your Score							
	Judges' Score							
Show 11	Your Score							
	Judges' Score							
Show 12	Your Score							
	Judges' Score							
The Final	Your Score							
	Judges' Score							
	Your Score							

JUDGE

Jerry & Anton	Nicky & Karen	Kimberley & Pasha	Richard & Erin	Lisa & Robin	Sid & Ola	Victoria & Brendan	Knocked Out
							Winner

SCD1 Natasha & Brendan
SCD2 Jill & Darren B
SCD3 Darren G & Lilya
SCD4 Mark & Karen
SCD5 Alesha & Matthew

SCD6 Tom & Camilla
SCD7 Chris & Ola
SCD8 Kara & Artem
SCD9 Harry & Aliona